T0209725

An Analysis of

G. E. M. Anscombe's

Modern Moral Philosophy

Jonny Blamey
with
Jon Thompson

Published by Macat International Ltd
24:13 Coda Centre, 189 Munster Road, London SW6 6AW.

Distributed exclusively by Routledge
2 Park Square, Milton Park, Abingdon, Oxon OX14 4RN
711 Third Avenue, New York, NY 10017, USA

Routledge is an imprint of the Taylor & Francis Group, an informa business

www.macat.com
info@macat.com

Cataloguing in Publication Data
A catalogue record for this book is available from the British Library.
Library of Congress Cataloguing-in-Publication Data is available upon request.
Cover illustration: Etienne Gilfillan

ISBN 978-1-912302-93-2 (hardback)
ISBN 978-1-912127-23-8 (paperback)
ISBN 978-1-912281-81-7 (e-book)

Notice

CONTENTS

THE MACAT LIBRARY

The Macat Library is a series of unique academic explorations of seminal works in the humanities and social sciences – books and papers that have had a significant and widely recognised impact on their disciplines. It has been created to serve as much more than just a summary of what lies between the covers of a great book. It illuminates and explores the influences on, ideas of, and impact of that book. Our goal is to offer a learning resource that encourages critical thinking and fosters a better, deeper understanding of important ideas.

Each publication is divided into three Sections: Influences, Ideas, and Impact. Each Section has four Modules. These explore every important facet of the work, and the responses to it.

This Section-Module structure makes a Macat Library book easy to use, but it has another important feature. Because each Macat book is written to the same format, it is possible (and encouraged!) to cross-reference multiple Macat books along the same lines of inquiry or research. This allows the reader to open up interesting interdisciplinary pathways.

To further aid your reading, lists of glossary terms and people mentioned are included at the end of this book (these are indicated by an asterisk [*] throughout) – as well as a list of works cited.

Macat has worked with the University of Cambridge to identify the elements of critical thinking and understand the ways in which six different skills combine to enable effective thinking.
Three allow us to fully understand a problem; three more give us the tools to solve it. Together, these six skills make up the **PACIER** model of critical thinking. They are:

ANALYSIS – understanding how an argument is built
EVALUATION – exploring the strengths and weaknesses of an argument
INTERPRETATION – understanding issues of meaning

CREATIVE THINKING – coming up with new ideas and fresh connections
PROBLEM-SOLVING – producing strong solutions
REASONING – creating strong arguments

To find out more, visit **WWW.MACAT.COM.**

CRITICAL THINKING AND "MODERN MORAL PHILOSOPHY"

Primary critical thinking skill: EVALUATION
Secondary critical thinking skill: ANALYSIS

Elizabeth Anscombe's 1958 essay "Modern Moral Philosophy" is a cutting intervention in modern philosophy that shows the full power of good evaluative and analytical critical thinking skills.

Though only 16 pages long, Anscombe's paper set out to do nothing less than reform the entire field of modern moral philosophy – something that could only be done by carefully examining the existing arguments of the giants of the field. To do this, she deployed the central skills of evaluation and analysis.

In critical thinking, analysis helps understand the sequence and features of arguments: it asks what reasons these arguments produce, what implicit reasons and assumptions they rely on, what conclusions they arrive at. Evaluation involves judging whether or not the arguments are strong enough to sustain their conclusions: it asks how acceptable, adequate, and relevant the reasons given are, and whether or not the conclusions drawn from them are really valid.

In "Modern Moral Philosophy," Anscombe dispassionately turns these skills on figures that have dominated moral philosophy since the 18th-century, revealing the underlying assumptions of their work, their weaknesses and strengths, and showing that in many ways the supposed differences between their arguments are actually negligible. A brilliantly incisive piece, "Modern Moral Philosophy" radically affected its field, remaining required – and controversial – reading today.

ABOUT THE AUTHOR OF THE ORIGINAL WORK

Elizabeth Anscombe —also known as G. E. M. Anscombe—was born in 1919, and was a major British philosopher of the twentieth century. She studied at Oxford and subsequently taught both there and at the University of Cambridge.

Anscombe was a follower of the celebrated Austrian philosopher Ludwig Wittgenstein and attended his lectures at Cambridge, later translating his work. A devout Roman Catholic, she was renowned not only for her philosophical work but also for her moral stance on several ethical and political issues, including opposition to contraception and nuclear weapons. She publicly opposed the honorary degree awarded by Oxford to US President Harry S. Truman on the grounds that he had approved the dropping of nuclear bombs on Japanese cities in World War II. Anscombe died in 2001 at the age of 81.

ABOUT THE AUTHORS OF THE ANALYSIS

Dr Jonny Blamey received his PhD in philosophy from King's College London. His work focuses on the philosophy of probability and epistemology.

Jon Thompson currently researches in the philosophy department at King's College London.

ABOUT MACAT

GREAT WORKS FOR CRITICAL THINKING

Macat is focused on making the ideas of the world's great thinkers accessible and comprehensible to everybody, everywhere, in ways that promote the development of enhanced critical thinking skills.

It works with leading academics from the world's top universities to produce new analyses that focus on the ideas and the impact of the most influential works ever written across a wide variety of academic disciplines. Each of the works that sit at the heart of its growing library is an enduring example of great thinking. But by setting them in context – and looking at the influences that shaped their authors, as well as the responses they provoked – Macat encourages readers to look at these classics and game-changers with fresh eyes. Readers learn to think, engage and challenge their ideas, rather than simply accepting them.

'Macat offers an amazing first-of-its-kind tool for interdisciplinary learning and research. Its focus on works that transformed their disciplines and its rigorous approach, drawing on the world's leading experts and educational institutions, opens up a world-class education to anyone.'

Andreas Schleicher
Director for Education and Skills, Organisation for Economic
Co-operation and Development

'Macat is taking on some of the major challenges in university education … They have drawn together a strong team of active academics who are producing teaching materials that are novel in the breadth of their approach.'

Prof Lord Broers,
former Vice-Chancellor of the University of Cambridge

'The Macat vision is exceptionally exciting. It focuses upon new modes of learning which analyse and explain seminal texts which have profoundly influenced world thinking and so social and economic development. It promotes the kind of critical thinking which is essential for any society and economy.
This is the learning of the future.'

Rt Hon Charles Clarke, former UK Secretary of State for Education

'The Macat analyses provide immediate access to the critical conversation surrounding the books that have shaped their respective discipline, which will make them an invaluable resource to all of those, students and teachers, working in the field.'

Professor William Tronzo, University of California at San Diego

WAYS IN TO THE TEXT

KEY POINTS

- G. E. M. Anscombe was a British philosopher best known for her writing on ethics*.

- Her paper "Modern Moral Philosophy" investigated notions such as moral obligation* in increasingly secular societies.

- Anscombe's text helped modernize moral philosophy and reevaluated ethics in contemporary philosophy.

Who Was G. E. M. Anscombe?

Elizabeth (G. E. M.) Anscombe, the author of the paper "Modern Moral Philosophy" (1958), was one of the most important and accomplished philosophers of the twentieth century. Her writing on ethics and moral philosophy was highly influential, and she pioneered contemporary action theory.*

Anscombe studied at Oxford University, obtaining a degree in Classics and Philosophy in 1941; later, she worked at Cambridge University, where she befriended the Austrian philosopher Ludwig Wittgenstein.* One of his most devoted students, she went on to translate his work. His influence on her was considerable: even after she returned to Oxford, she traveled back to Cambridge on a weekly basis to attend his lectures. Like Wittgenstein, Anscombe is known for her sharp analytic insights.

Anscombe is known for her strong Roman Catholic* beliefs, her conservative views on sexual ethics, and her long-held opposition to nuclear arms. Controversially, she opposed contraception and homosexual acts. Her views inspired the creation of a student organization promoting chastity and traditional sexual values—the Anscombe Society, which established branches at Princeton, MIT, and several other universities. She staunchly opposed the use of atomic weapons at the end of World War II and, in 1956, she publicly criticized Oxford University's decision to award an honorary degree to US president Harry S. Truman,* citing his approval of the nuclear bombing of the Japanese cities of Hiroshima and Nagasaki.* This action was indefensible, Anscombe believed, because, even if it had brought an immediate end to the war and reduced the total number of lives lost, it was aimed at killing innocent civilians.

What Does "Modern Moral Philosophy" Say?

Anscombe's most important work is her paper "Modern Moral Philosophy." From the outset, she identifies that the paper contains "three theses":[1] that concepts of moral obligation were irrelevant in a secular society; that there were virtually no differences between the major British moral philosophers (that is, the consequentialists,* who judged the moral value of an action from its consequences); and that without an "adequate philosophy of psychology,"[2] moral philosophy becomes a fruitless field of study.

In her first point, Anscombe proposes that some ideas are the remnants of a Christian tradition that alone can issue moral laws. These include moral obligation and duty and the distinction between actions that are morally right and those that are morally wrong. A firm believer in God, Anscombe does not dispute divine power but, rather, argues that a secular society can no longer use the language of ethics. The word "ought," for instance, or related notions such as moral obligation (things we are obliged to do on the grounds of morality), could not be used because secular societies, by their very nature, were detached from God.

"Ought" denotes the command of a moral authority, which, in the past, would have been God. In a secular society, though, God is no longer the sole voice of authority able to command us to behave in certain ways. Without this connection to God, she argues, such words and concepts have lost their meaning.

Anscombe's second proposition is that it is impossible to distinguish between the English moral philosophers of the previous 75 years. There was no genuine debate going on in moral philosophy, she claims, and all its proponents had uniformly rejected God and fundamentally agreed on consequentialism— the view that any action is only morally relevant in terms of its foreseeable consequences, and any rules of behavior can in some circumstances be broken. Though supposedly different from one another, all contemporary moral philosophies lead, she argued, to this kind of position—a view that, ultimately, could be used to defend the execution of an innocent person.

If someone with a gun told you that she would kill 20 innocent people unless you killed one innocent person (and you had good reason to believe her), according to the consequentialist position it would be right for you to kill the innocent person and wrong for you to fail to kill the innocent person since the consequences of killing the innocent person are preferable to those of not killing her.[3] This was completely at odds with the Christian morality that had dominated Europe for more than 1,000 years, according to which certain actions were immoral, regardless of their consequences.

Finally, she suggests that moral philosophy needs an alternative model, based on psychology. She argues that there can be no interpretation of moral right and wrong that excludes God, and ethics can no longer be based on divine rules. Instead, Anscombe suggests returning to secular concepts of practical reasoning, virtue, and justice derived from the work of the ancient Greek philosopher Aristotle.* So, instead of an action being morally wrong, it would be unjust. Virtue ethics*—an approach to ethics that identifies the good life in terms of attaining, and acting in accord with, virtues such as justice, wisdom and generosity—could exist in a non-moral sense and without the need for divine authority.

Why Does "Modern Moral Philosophy" Matter?

Anscombe made highly acclaimed contributions to many topics, including action theory (a subfield of philosophy that analyzes the nature of human action), metaphysics* (the study of the ultimate nature of reality), and the work of Wittgenstein. Her essay "Modern Moral Philosophy" matters, in particular, because of its lasting impact on ethics. It helped revive the school of moral philosophy called virtue ethics and many later philosophers took up the conceptual and moral problems it raised. A few of the most important include the English philosopher Philippa Foot* in *Virtues and Vices and Other Essays*,[4] the influential Scottish philosopher Alasdair MacIntyre* in *After Virtue*,[5] and the prominent virtue ethicist Rosalind Hursthouse* of the University of Auckland in *On Virtue Ethics*.[6]

More fundamentally, Anscombe's text tackles such questions as the importance of acting ethically and the value of ethics to philosophy. She suggests that there is not much point in doing moral philosophy unless important concepts such as obligation, justice, and virtue are completely understood. The text demands a new, clearer thinking and calls for philosophers to explain their terms and concepts properly.

Anscombe's essay helped reform moral philosophy. In it, she attacked consequentialism and ethics derived from the work of the influential German philosopher Immanuel Kant,* describing them as immoral or simply incoherent. She challenged the consequentialist position that condemning the innocent to death could be the "right" thing to do if it could have some positive effect overall. She described this idea as corrupt, believing that a wider, universal human morality could not depend on fluctuating majority decisions.

In a contemporary world accustomed to mounting civilian deaths in international conflicts carried out in the name of the greater good, Anscombe's account of morality offers a radical alternative. This alternative places weight on the justice or wisdom or temperance of actions themselves, rather than on their consequences.

NOTES

1   G. E. M. Anscombe, "Modern Moral Philosophy," *Philosophy* 33, no. 124 (1958): 1.

2   Anscombe, "Modern Moral Philosophy," 1.

3   This example is from Bernard Williams and J. J. C. Smart, *Utilitarianism: For and Against* (Cambridge: Cambridge University Press, 1973), 97–116.

4   Philippa Foot, *Virtues and Vices and Other Essays in Moral Philosophy* (Berkeley and Los Angeles: University of California Press, 1978).

5   See Alasdair MacIntyre, *After Virtue*, 3rd revised edition (London: Duckworth, 2007).

6   See Rosalind Hursthouse, *On Virtue Ethics* (Oxford: Oxford University Press, 2001).

SECTION 1
INFLUENCES

THE AUTHOR AND THE HISTORICAL CONTEXT

KEY POINTS

- "Modern Moral Philosophy" transformed moral philosophy.* It criticized the consequentialist* position that an action's morality should be judged on its consequences and the ethical philosophy derived from the German thinker Immanuel Kant* for relying on a defunct concept of moral obligation* (a requirement upon an individual to do something or refrain from doing something). In their place, it offered an alternative moral theory, now known as virtue ethics,* which emphasizes acting in accordance with such virtues as justice, prudence, and temperance (moderation).

- Elizabeth (G. E. M.) Anscombe was a practicing Roman Catholic* who worked at Oxford and Cambridge universities during a high point in analytic philosophy* (a set of philosophical methods that focus on the analysis of language and concepts). She was a favorite student of the influential Austrian thinker Ludwig Wittgenstein* and collated, edited, and translated his work.

- Writing in the aftermath of World War II,* injustices perpetrated by the Allies—the forces led by Britain and the United States—especially the atomic bombs dropped by the United States on two Japanese cities, provoked Anscombe to criticize the consequentialist morality then prevalent.

> **❝ It is not possible for us at present to do moral philosophy. ❞**
>
> G. E. M. Anscombe, "Modern Moral Philosophy"

Why Read This Text?

G. E. M. Anscombe's paper "Modern Moral Philosophy"[1] was published in the journal *Philosophy* in 1958. In it, Anscombe challenges the very foundations of moral philosophy (inquiry into ethics)* as it was practiced at the time. She argues that there is no point in moral philosophy until the important concepts—obligation, justice, and virtue—are sufficiently analyzed and understood, and points a finger at contemporary moral philosophers who, she says, use these notions without any clear meaning. She highlights the concept of "moral obligation" or "moral ought," claiming that they came from a conception of ethics derived from divine law—but this had long been abandoned by philosophers as a historical product of Christianity.

In other words, as Christianity was gradually abandoned in philosophical circles, the concept of moral obligation became increasingly meaningless. Philosophers were using words that, essentially, had lost their meaning.

Anscombe also invented the term "consequentialist" to describe the philosophical view that a moral judgment can only ever be made about an action by examining its expected consequences. She raises serious objections both to this idea and to Kantian ethics,* which held, in short, that an action is moral if and only if you could make it into a universal law. So, for Kant, telling falsehoods was wrong because it is impossible rationally to will that everyone everywhere should always tell falsehoods.

Finally, Anscombe's essay is also very important because it launched the ideas that would become the discipline of virtue ethics.

Author's Life

Gertrude Elizabeth Margaret Anscombe was the daughter of a schoolmaster and a Classics scholar. She was educated at Sydenham College and as a teenager read a great deal of philosophy and theology, becoming a convinced Roman Catholic* as a result. Anscombe studied at Oxford University, where she obtained a degree in Classics and Philosophy in 1941. After undergraduate studies, she pursued a career as an academic philosopher at both Oxford and Cambridge. She would go on to hold the chair in philosophy at the University of Cambridge from 1970 to 1986, and her most important philosophical works are "Modern Moral Philosophy" (1958), *Intention* (1957), and *Causality and Determination* (1971).[2]

Anscombe wrote "Modern Moral Philosophy" in 1958 while a research fellow at Somerville College, Oxford. She had been a student and close friend of the highly influential Austrian thinker Ludwig Wittgenstein,* and became an executor of his work after his death in 1951; Wittgenstein's influence can be seen throughout Anscombe's other major works, including "Modern Moral Philosophy." She was married to another Catholic philosopher, Peter T. Geach,* with whom she had seven children. In addition to her philosophical papers, of which "Modern Moral Philosophy" is among the most important, Anscombe wrote several papers specifically for a Roman Catholic readership.

Anscombe was a famously independent philosopher. She gained some notoriety when, in 1956, she publicly objected to the honorary degree that Oxford University awarded to US President Harry S. Truman.* Her grounds were that he had been responsible for the nuclear bombing and mass killing of the people of the Japanese cities of Hiroshima and Nagasaki* during World War II. It had been argued by some that Truman's action was acceptable because, though the bombs killed hundreds of thousands of Japanese citizens, it probably prevented even more deaths of US and Japanese soldiers.

Anscombe did not consider this a legitimate action, however, because even if it brought the war to an immediate end, its aim was to kill innocent civilians.

Author's Background

Perhaps the most relevant social factor behind Anscombe's essay is the social progressivism* of the post-World War II period of British history. Progressivism tended to remove long-standing moral prohibitions such as the rule against bombing civilians as a means of shortening the war. The justification for this was that, by lifting such restrictions, the world's total suffering would be minimized and its total pleasure maximized. Anscombe cited these attitudes in her radio address "Does Oxford Moral Philosophy Corrupt the Youth?",[3] convinced that some actions are categorically wrong in their own right.

This makes Anscombe a moral absolutist. She argues that Oxford moral philosophy is not responsible for corrupting youth—it is merely a reflection of the social current of progressivism: "This philosophy is conceived perfectly in the spirit of the time and might be called the philosophy of the flattery of that spirit."[4] Anscombe's condemnation of progressivism rests on what she sees as the purpose of moral philosophy: to teach students to question popular ethical trends. This, she said, was something her colleagues utterly failed to do.

NOTES

1   G. E. M. Anscombe, "Modern Moral Philosophy," *Philosophy* 33, no. 124 (1958): 1–19.

2   See G. E. M. Anscombe, "Modern Moral Philosophy"; Anscombe, *Intention* (Oxford: Blackwell, 1957); and Anscombe, *Causality and Determination: An Inaugural Lecture* (Cambridge: Cambridge University Press, 1971).

3 G. E. M. Anscombe, "Does Oxford Moral Philosophy Corrupt the Youth?",
   in *Human Life, Action and Ethics*, St. Andrews Studies in Philosophy
   and Public Policy, ed. Mary Geach and Luke Gormally (Exeter: Imprint
   Academic, 2005), Kindle edition; originally printed in *The Listener* 57
   (February 14, 1957): 266–7, 271. The question posed to Anscombe in
   the title is a reference to ancient Athenian philosopher Socrates,* who
   was executed on the charge of "corrupting the youth" when, in fact, he
   was merely training them to question the prevailing cultural assumptions
   of the time.

4 Anscombe, "Does Oxford Moral Philosophy Corrupt the Youth?", Kindle
   edition.

MODULE 2
ACADEMIC CONTEXT

KEY POINTS

- Moral philosophy is concerned with understanding what it is to be moral and how such terms as "right" and "wrong" should be used.

- Moral philosophy has four broad approaches: consequentialism,* which focuses solely on the consequences of an action; Kantian ethics,* which focuses on an individual deciding on his or her own moral rules; divine command ethics,* which focuses on obedience to God's law; and virtue ethics,* which focuses on understanding and developing the virtues.*

- Anscombe regarded consequentialism as deeply morally problematic. She proposed instead a return to the Aristotelian approach to ethics* bolstered by psychology.

The Work in its Context

In "Modern Moral Philosophy," G. E. M. Anscombe surveys and critiques the main moral philosophies of the 1950s.

Moral philosophy deals with such themes as the nature of moral obligation* (a requirement upon an individual to do something or refrain from doing something), right action, and the good life. What is the purpose of life? "Consequentialism" (a term Anscombe invented) is the view that, morally speaking, only consequences matter. In other words, rules or prohibitions or divine commands are irrelevant, unless they contribute to good consequences. But in that case, it is the consequence—and not the rule or command—that makes the action morally good. A subdivision of consequentialism is

> ❖ "Modern Moral Philosophy" also touched a nerve with philosophers who advocated one or the other of the condemned views. One reason for this was the rather dismissive or moralistic tone she took in some of her criticisms. ❖
>
> Julia Driver, "Gertrude Elizabeth Margaret Anscombe," in *Stanford Encyclopedia of Philosophy*

utilitarianism,* which argues that only the production of pleasure and reduction of pain make an action moral.

The leading contemporary alternative to consequentialism was Kantian ethics, an approach that originated from the thought of the eighteenth-century German philosopher Immanuel Kant.* Kant highlights duties: norms or rules chosen for their own sake and not for their consequences; for him, duty underlies the morality of any action.

Divine command ethics is a form of morality that assumes the existence of a divinity who makes the rules we must obey; this is the approach of Christian morality.

Finally, virtue ethics was the preferred moral view in the classical world. Ancient Greek and Roman philosophers believed that the aim of ethics was the development and practice of the virtues (dispositions of character that are expressed in human action—such as temperance, wisdom, and courage).

Overview of the Field

Consequentialism (usually known as utilitarianism) was an idea famously developed by the English philosopher and social reformer Jeremy Bentham.* In his 1789 book *An Introduction to the Principles of Morals and Legislation*[1] he famously argued that pleasure and pain are the two competing masters of humanity—they "govern us in all we do, in all we say, in all we think."[2] Bentham also suggested a calculus to determine the morality of an action according to how much pleasure it would produce and how much pain it would prevent or alleviate. Bentham's student, the philosopher John Stuart Mill, further developed this theory* in his influential 1861 book *Utilitarianism*.

According to Immanuel Kant, the originator of Kantian ethics, the individual "legislates" moral norms for him- or herself, based on what any rational person would do in a given situation. This is known as the "categorical imperative." As an example, Kant (and later "Kantians") have believed that a rational person would choose never to lie. This is because, if I were to lie in order to, say, swindle you out of money, then I would be implicitly endorsing others lying to me when it was to their financial advantage. We would lose the capacity to distinguish between truth and falsehood, and live in a contradictory, muddled fashion—something no rational thinker would choose.

The Greek philosopher Aristotle* is the most important figure in virtue ethics. The author of the influential *Nicomachean Ethics*, Aristotle saw the good life as being characterized by a particular kind of happiness called *eudaimonia* (Greek for "blessedness"). *Eudaimonia* is the ultimate good for human beings, and it is achieved by perfecting such virtues as courage, wisdom, temperance, and so on. Aristotle's virtue ethics, however, should not be thought of as focusing on "being good" as a mental state. On the contrary, "doing right actions" is the key to Aristotle's belief in "virtuous activity."[3]

Academic Influences

Anscombe was undoubtedly inspired by the twentieth-century philosopher Ludwig Wittgenstein,* who was at that time enormously influential on the philosophical thinking at Oxford and Cambridge universities. Anscombe was one of his graduate students, and she translated his *Philosophical Investigations* into English.[4] Wittgenstein influenced Anscombe's criticism of concepts like "ought" and "obligation." He had famously argued that "the meaning of a word is its use in the language."[5] Anscombe continually questions the meaning of such moral words as "obligation" and "ought" in common usage as these are words that referred to the rules of a divine lawgiver (God).

While Wittgenstein influenced Anscombe in the area of philosophical methodology and analysis of language, it is Aristotle who is probably Anscombe's most important influence in the field of moral philosophy. In the text, Anscombe contrasts all forms of modern moral philosophy with Aristotle's and proposes giving moral philosophy back its coherence by reviving the notion of the virtues, arguing: "Eventually it might be possible to advance to considering the concept of a virtue; with which, I suppose, we should be beginning some sort of study of ethics."[6]

In short, such rich concepts as "justice" or "prudence" could do the philosophical work that the words "ought" and "morally wrong" were employed to do in modern philosophy.

NOTES

1   Jeremy Bentham, *An Introduction to the Principles of Morals and Legislation* (Oxford: Clarendon Press, 1907).

2   Jeremy Bentham, *Principles of Morals and Legislation*, 1; quoted in Julia Driver, "The History of Utilitarianism," *Stanford Encyclopedia of Philosophy* (Winter 2014 edition), ed. Edward N. Zalta, accessed October 6, 2015, http://plato.stanford.edu/entries/utilitarianism-history/.

3   Aristotle, *Nicomachean Ethics,* ed. and trans. Roger Crisp (Cambridge: Cambridge University Press, 2014), ix, 12.

4   Ludwig Wittgenstein, *Philosophical Investigations* (*Philosophische Untersuchungen) English & German*, trans. G. E. M. Anscombe (Oxford: Basil Blackwell, 1953).

5   Ludwig Wittgenstein, *Philosophical Investigations*, 4th edition, 2009, ed. and trans. P. M. S. Hacker and Joachim Schulte (Oxford: Wiley-Blackwell, 2009), 43.

6   G. E. M. Anscombe, "Modern Moral Philosophy," *Philosophy* 33, no. 124 (1958): 12–13.

MODULE 3
THE PROBLEM

KEY POINTS

- The key question in G. E. M. Anscombe's "Modern Moral Philosophy" is: what is the nature and meaning of moral obligation?*

- For consequentialism,* we are morally obliged to do whatever results in the best consequences; ethical anti-realism* contends that there are no moral facts or obligations.

- Anscombe proposed abandoning consequentialism because the idea of "moral obligation" was a hangover from the concept of divine laws, a concept in which people no longer generally believed.

Core Question

G. E. M. Anscombe's central inquiry in "Modern Moral Philosophy" is into the nature and meaning of moral obligation. She raised the question in a provocative and unique way, arguing that moral obligation and the moral "ought" had no meaning in the philosophical discourse of her day. Anscombe strongly opposed the consequentialist justifications of what she considered morally outrageous acts such as the atomic bombing of the Japanese cities of Hiroshima and Nagasaki* by US President Harry S. Truman* at the end of World War II; the killing of hundreds of thousands of innocent civilians could be justified by consequentialist thought so long as it saved more lives in the long run. Anscombe believed such thinking was utterly out of step with traditional morality.

Consequentialists had answered the question of moral obligation

> **❝** My mother settled down to read the standard modern ethicists and was appalled. The thing these people had in common, which had made Truman drop the bomb and dons defend him, was a belief which Anscombe called 'consequentialism.' **❞**
>
> Mary Geach, Introduction to *Human Life, Action and Ethics: Essays by G. E. M. Anscombe*

by reducing it solely to a matter of consequences. Anscombe, however, observed that this sense of moral obligation has no direct parallel in either the language or the moral philosophy of the Greek philosopher Aristotle.* She suggested that the concept of moral obligation is a residue of a Christian belief in divine legislative authority: because of God's supreme power, authority, and wisdom, we must behave morally. But, argues Anscombe, consequentialists do not believe in God, or, if they do, they do not believe that divine authority creates our moral obligations. As a result, they use the concept of "moral obligation" without explaining its meaning. Anscombe proposes that moral philosophers jettison "obligation" and "ought" as leftovers from Christian morality and instead use richer virtue concepts like justice and temperance.

The Participants

Anscombe's essay focuses on the state of moral philosophy in the first half of the twentieth century. Two of Anscombe's British predecessors are key to understanding the context in which she was writing.

The first of these, Henry Sidgwick,* was the foremost British philosopher of the Victorian period (1837–1901).* His most influential work in moral philosophy was *Methods of Ethics* (1874), a culmination of the utilitarian* ethical tradition (the approach to moral philosophy according to which the best action is the one that produces the greatest happiness in the greatest number). According to historians, Sidgwick "set the agenda for most of the twentieth-century debates between utilitarians and their critics."[1] He was a unique thinker in his time and tried to combine utilitarianism with Immanuel Kant's* deontology* (an ethical philosophy founded on the notion of duty) to form a theory he called ethical "intuitionism."* Sidgwick argues that, while we have certain intuitions about our duty in a particular situation, those intuitions about morality eventually collapse into utilitarian principles. So an individual may intuitively perceive the duty not to strike an innocent stranger in the street, but the ultimate principle that makes such an action wrong is a utilitarian principle of preventing suffering. By implication, the principle that one should not strike a stranger can be overturned in the light of the good consequences it may bring about in the end.

The second important predecessor, British philosopher G. E. Moore,* continued Sidgwick's combination of intuitionism and utilitarianism. A highly influential thinker, Moore was a fellow of Trinity College, Cambridge, and author of the voluminous *Principia Ethica* (1903). In *Principia*, he argued that "good" was not a natural property—that to identify "good" with any natural thing was to commit the "naturalistic fallacy."* In other words, it is always an open question whether any particular natural thing or natural fact is good. Moore concludes that the property "good" cannot exist independently of natural objects or states of affairs. In other words, the property of goodness is like the property of red: though redness is perceived in certain objects because of their physical characteristics, redness is distinct from those physical properties.

These two philosophers helped lay the groundwork for moral philosophy in Anscombe's day in two ways. First, they held to consequentialism in some form. Second, they created a gap between the natural facts of the world and the concepts "ought" and "right" and "obligation." For them, no everyday fact—like "the child is thirsty"—entails any particular moral injunction such as "I should give the child water."

The Contemporary Debate

In preparation for teaching a moral philosophy class at Oxford University in 1958, Anscombe made a survey of the modern moral philosophers. She seems to have started with the eighteenth-century Scottish philosopher David Hume* and Immanuel Kant, and continued with Sidgwick, Moore, and her own contemporaries. All of these philosophers shared a tendency to divide completely the "moral" sphere from the "natural" sphere. Hume had argued that there is no logical link between "is" statements and "ought" statements. So, for instance, the factual statement "God commands you to honor your parents" does not lead to the moral statement "You ought to honor your parents" because there is an unstated premise in between: "You ought to do whatever God commands."

This unstated premise already has an "ought" and so is a moral, rather than a factual, statement. Hume is pointing out a gap between the normal world of facts and the special world of "moral oughts."[2]

In this context, Anscombe cast a skeptical eye over all these thinkers, and applied to their moral philosophies the linguistic analysis she had learned from Ludwig Wittgenstein.* She concluded that, if words like "ought" and "obligation" gain their meaning by their relation to God, then they lost that meaning when they were used without it.

NOTES

1   Barton Schultz, "Henry Sidgwick," *The Stanford Encyclopedia of Philosophy* (Summer 2015 edition), ed. Edward N. Zalta, accessed October 7, 2015, http://plato.stanford.edu/archives/sum2015/entries/sidgwick/.

2   David Hume, *Treatise of Human Nature*, ed. L. A. Selby-Bigge and P. H. Nidditch, 2nd edition (Oxford: Oxford University Press, 1978), 469–70.

MODULE 4
THE AUTHOR'S CONTRIBUTION

KEY POINTS

- Anscombe argued that moral obligation* is a leftover from a system of morality based on divine authority in which people no longer believed—therefore the concept should be dropped.

- This paved the way for virtue ethics,* an alternative to consequentialism* that focused on the virtues: justice and temperance, for example.

- Anscombe was influenced by the philosopher Wittgenstein's* linguistic analysis and applied it to the concept of moral obligation.

Author's Aims

The original groundbreaking idea in G. E. M. Anscombe's "Modern Moral Philosophy" is that the current "moral" sense of such terms as "ought," "obligation," "right and wrong," and "duty" is incoherent and arguably unnecessary. This sense of "moral" did not exist at all in the work of the Greek philosopher Aristotle,* who focused instead on the nature of the virtues—such as courage, justice, wisdom, and temperance—and their role in a flourishing human life. The absence of moral obligation in Aristotle's writings shows that a coherent theory of ethics does not need such a concept.

The notion of moral obligation is also, Anscombe argues, incoherent. She puts forward the hypothesis that the concept arose as a by-product of the 2,000 years or so of Christianity that came between Aristotle and the twentieth century. Its meaning depends, she says, on a belief in a divine legislator (God) because a superior power and authority

> **❝** First … it is not profitable at present for us to do moral philosophy … Second … the concepts of obligation, and duty—*moral* obligation and *moral* duty, that is to say … ought to be jettisoned if this is psychologically possible … Third … the differences between the well-known English writers on moral philosophy from Sidgwick to the present day are of little importance. **❞**
>
> G. E. M. Anscombe, "Modern Moral Philosophy"

is needed both to create a "law" and to enforce "obligations." So, for instance, the "law of the land" works because it is enacted by an entire nation, lending it the means to punish me for disobedience. Anscombe seems to suggest that there is a similar connection between God and moral obligation. This presented moral philosophers with a choice: either return to a religious conception of ethics or abandon talk of "ought" or "obligation" in favor of richer concepts like "justice," "virtues," "vice," and so on. This was unprecedented.

Approach

Anscombe's main aims in "Modern Moral Philosophy" are philosophical and public. Philosophically, the paper takes both an analytic approach, with its emphasis on language and definitions, and a historical approach. While Anscombe is interested in challenging the meaning of words like "ought," she is also interested in clarifying moral concepts. She uses Aristotle's moral philosophy as a foil against modern authors, writing: "Anyone who has read Aristotle's *Ethics* and has also read modern moral philosophy must be struck by the great contrasts between them."[1] While a historical approach to moral philosophy was not new, Anscombe's innovation was to apply Aristotle's thought to modern moral questions.

Anscombe had wider concerns, too, particularly what she viewed as a general moral decline in civic society. It stemmed, she believed, from consequentialism, which gave license to any kind of action, however seemingly immoral, on the grounds of its foreseeable consequences. In "Mr. Truman's Degree" (1958),[2] Anscombe argued that US president Harry S. Truman* had committed mass murder by authorizing the use of the atom bomb on the Japanese cities of Hiroshima and Nagasaki. Similarly, in "Does Oxford Philosophy Corrupt the Youth?" (1957), she claims that consequentialism has resulted in a mentality conducive to oppression: "Preventative measures means they want to go into people's homes and push them around not because they have 'done anything,' but just in case they do."[3]

Her worries about consequentialism clearly reach far beyond philosophy and into the problematic arena of public morality.

Contribution in Context

Anscombe was undoubtedly influenced by the philosopher Ludwig Wittgenstein and is sometimes referred to as his disciple.[4] She worked with the ordinary-language method that was popular at the time and can in part be traced to Wittgenstein, who seems to have believed that the way we use language ultimately gives words their meanings.

Anscombe uses this idea in the following way.

First, the concepts of "obligation" and "moral ought' were essentially borrowed from Jewish and Christian theology and adapted to Western philosophy under Christianity. The words gained their meaning, implies Anscombe, through their use in relation to God. However, after people have dismissed the concept of God, it is unclear in what sense "moral obligation" is used. We see this in Anscombe's treatment of the philosopher Immanuel Kant's* "categorical imperative";* for Kant, we are obligated to do the right thing because we can legislate for ourselves. According to Anscombe, however, Kant is simply borrowing a word that has only had meaning because of its use in relation to God; Kant's use empties it of all meaning.

NOTES

1   G. E. M. Anscombe, "Modern Moral Philosophy," *Philosophy* 33, no. 124 (1958): 1.

2   G. E. M. Anscombe, "Mr. Truman's Degree," in *Ethics, Religion and Politics* (Oxford: Basil Blackwell, 1981).

3   G. E. M. Anscombe, "Does Oxford Moral Philosophy Corrupt the Youth?", in *Human Life, Action and Ethics*, St. Andrews Studies in Philosophy and Public Policy, ed. Mary Geach and Luke Gormally (Exeter: Imprint Academic, 2005), Kindle edition.

4   Peter J. Conradi, *Iris Murdoch: A Life* (London: HarperCollins, 2002), 266: "Since [Iris Murdoch] was too late to hear Wittgenstein lecture, his influence reached her mainly through disciples such as Elizabeth Anscombe."

SECTION 2
IDEAS

MAIN IDEAS

KEY POINTS

- Anscombe's key themes are consequentialism,* ethical philosophy derived from the thought of the philosopher Immanuel Kant* (Kantian ethics),* moral obligation,* a law conception of ethics,* the Aristotelian approach to ethics,* and the virtues.*

- All modern moral philosophy, she argues, uses a concept of moral obligation that makes no sense without a belief in a God who makes moral laws.

- Anscombe argued that all modern moral philosophy was essentially the same—consequentialist. Consequentialism, she says, is not only conceptually confused, but also morally dangerous because it justifies immoral acts.

Key Themes

There are four primary themes in G. E. M. Anscombe's "Modern Moral Philosophy."

- The intelligibility question: in what sense can moral philosophers' current uses of "morally ought," "right," "wrong" and "obligation" be understood without belief in God?
- A plausible moral theory must be coherent and must not be immoral.
- Consequentialism, Kantianism, and contractualism* all fall short of these first two criteria in some way.

> ❝ Anscombe's ... theses are the following: (1) the *profitability claim*: it is not at present profitable for us to do moral philosophy; (2) the *conceptual claim*: the concepts of 'moral obligation', 'moral duty,' what is 'morally right and wrong,' and 'ought' in its moral sense should be discarded; (3) the *triviality claim*: the differences between English moral philosophers since Sidgwick are of little significance. ❞
>
> Roger Crisp, "Does Moral Philosophy Rest on a Mistake?"

- There is a great divide between the ancient Greek philosopher Aristotle's* virtue ethics* and all ethical theories of moral philosophy formulated since the 1700s.

Together, these themes create a single, very deep, and multifaceted question: what is the meaning of moral terms like "ought," "right," and "obligation" for modern philosophers who reject belief in God? Among the possible answers she considers are that a) the will of society provides the grounding for "obligation," b) that self-legislation ("laws" made and observed by the self) provides it, or c) that consequences provide it.

Each of these answers, Anscombe argues, is either incoherent as a ground for the meaning of the word "ought" or is morally unacceptable. In contrast, she examines the virtue ethics of Aristotle, an approach founded on the observance of rich—or "thick"—values and concepts such as "wisdom," "courage," "justice," "truthfulness," "temperance" that require neither the "ought" and "obligation" concepts nor a divine legislator. Moral philosophers, Anscombe continues, are faced with a dilemma: either return to some form of belief in a divine legislator and keep notions of "ought" or pursue some version of Aristotle's virtue ethics.

Exploring the Ideas

First, it should be said that Anscombe does not argue that nonbelievers cannot use concepts like "moral obligation" and "ought." Instead, she says that, because these concepts originally gained their meaning by reference to God's law or God's commands, it is up to those who deny God's existence to explain the words' meaning and use.

Anscombe goes on to explore the most promising possible explanations of the concept of moral obligation—Kantianism, contractualism, and consequentialism—and she finds each, in turn, lacking.

The basic idea of Kantian ethics—the idea of legislating for oneself—is, she believes, incoherent. Kant had emphasized the individual's autonomy (self-rule) as his or her guiding ethical principle. But lawmaking, says Anscombe, requires a greater power or authority to govern a lesser power: "The concept of legislation requires superior power in the legislator."[1] So, in the political realm, a body such as a parliament or congress legislates, and the laws it passes are imposed on individuals who should then obey them. But since an individual cannot be both the legislator and the one legislated to, the analogy with political lawmaking does not hold.

Anscombe dismisses contractualism for moral, rather than strictly conceptual, reasons. Contractualism refers to any theory of morality that posits an implicit contract between members of a community that is supposed to ground moral obligation. If we must obey whichever moral norms the majority happens to choose, she argues, we will inevitably be subject to grossly unjust obligations. For example, if the majority were to choose tomorrow that races must be "kept pure" by preventing interracial marriage, it is difficult to see how contractualists could avoid making that a binding moral obligation.

Finally, Anscombe sees several flaws in consequentialism (any moral philosophy that defines the moral value of an action solely in terms of its consequences). Classical consequentialists assumed, she says, that they had a definite concept of pleasure; it was never established, however, whether pleasure was an internal impression or whether it was intrinsically tied up with the cause of that impression. Our language shows this, since we classify as pleasure both *feelings* ("There's a pleasant feeling in my arm") and *activities* ("Throwing a baseball is one of my pleasures.") Even if pleasure is an internal impression that all pleasant activities have in common, she continues, then choosing actions based on their pleasing consequences alone leads to disastrous moral results.

To illustrate this point Anscombe argues that judicious punishment of the innocent offers a model of injustice. But consequentialism cannot decide beforehand the morality of an unjust act like punishing the innocent: if a judge knows that condemning one innocent person to death will—for some reason— end up saving several other innocent lives, then that consequence means that the judge is morally obligated to condemn the innocent to death.

She argues that both divine law ethics* and Aristotelian ethics* determine that it is wrong to be unjust, whereas consequentialists will always allow circumstances in which it is right to commit such an unjust act.

Language and Expression

Anscombe was one of the greatest analytic philosophers* of the twentieth century, following a philosophical method that focuses on detailed conceptual and linguistic analysis.[2] So a good student of the text will pay attention both to her careful analysis and to her moral insight. Anscombe uses words in ways that can seem idiosyncratic to contemporary readers or nonphilosophers. For instance, "modern" describes philosophers roughly from the 1600s to her day—a broader range than is usually covered by "modern."

Anscombe coined the term "consequentialism"* in "Modern

Moral Philosophy"; it has subsequently become the most common term for moral theories that base the rightness of an act upon consequences alone. She also reintroduced the philosophical use of the term "virtue"; virtue ethics or Aristotelianism is now considered an alternative to Kantianism and consequentialism.

While Anscombe's essay is aimed at a philosophical audience rather than a popular one, her paper "Does Oxford Moral Philosophy Corrupt the Youth?", which displays certain parallels to "Modern Moral Philosophy," works on a more popular level. Anscombe's writing is notoriously dense. Her daughter once remarked: "Her style is dense and unrepetitive, and it is hard to know sometimes whether it would be more clarificatory to go on to the next sentence, or to return to the previous one."[3] However, Anscombe is a very systematic thinker and defines words and concepts as she goes, and while she uses specialist language or examples, it is not in order to cloud her meaning but rather to illuminate it.

NOTES

1   G. E. M. Anscombe, "Modern Moral Philosophy," *Philosophy* 33, no. 124 (1958): 2.

2   Peter J. Conradi, *Iris Murdoch: A Life* (London: HarperCollins, 2002), 283: "The most brilliant of her generation of British philosophers, Elizabeth Anscombe was from 1946 a Research Fellow at Somerville."

3   Mary Geach, "Introduction," in G. E. M. Anscombe, "Does Oxford Moral Philosophy Corrupt the Youth?", in *Human Life, Action and Ethics*, St. Andrews Studies in Philosophy and Public Policy, ed. Mary Geach and Luke Gormally (Exeter: Imprint Academic, 2005), Kindle edition.

MODULE 6
SECONDARY IDEAS

KEY POINTS

- "Modern Moral Philosophy" has four main secondary ideas that together form the kernel of Anscombe's key objections to consequentialism.*

- She framed these key objections from the new perspective of virtue ethics*—an approach to moral philosophy that draws on the ethics of the ancient Greek philosopher Aristotle.

- Anscombe's account of intention and the description of actions has had a major impact upon action theory*— a subfield of philosophy that analyzes the nature of human action, inquiring into the mind, determinism,* and free will.

Other Ideas

There are four secondary themes in G. E. M. Anscombe's "Modern Moral Philosophy":

- The difference between foreseen consequences and intended consequences.
- The idea of an action as intended "under a description."
- The relationship between "ought" and "is."
- The return of rich concepts in ethics (like "virtue," "justice," and "truthfulness"), as opposed to blanket moral concepts such as "wrong," "ought," and the like.

Discussing the first of these themes, Anscombe points out that consequentialists such as the English philosopher Henry Sidgwick,*

> **❝ A man is responsible for the bad consequences of his bad actions, but gets no credit for the good ones; and contrariwise is not responsible for the bad consequences of good actions. ❞**
>
> G. E. M. Anscombe "Modern Moral Philosophy"

who subscribe to a moral philosophy that defines the moral value of an action solely in terms of its consequences, suppose that all *foreseen* consequences are *intended* consequences. Sidgwick "defines intention," Anscombe summarizes, "in such a way that one must be said to intend any foreseen consequences of one's voluntary action."[1] She argues that some foreseen consequences are not intended.

A second and related argument concerns whether an action is "intended under a description." By this phrase, Anscombe essentially means that an action is both intentional and intended as an action of injustice or murder or callousness. That is, it is both intended and the person performing the action has taken all relevant circumstances into account in his or her understanding of the action.

Anscombe also argues that it simply is not the case that an "ought" cannot be derived from an "is," as the eighteenth-century Scottish philosopher David Hume* had argued, and that it is easier to decide whether or not an action is unjust or callous than to decide whether it is "morally wrong." From the perspective of virtue ethics, however, it might be relatively easy to decide in a particular case whether an act was callous, for instance.

Exploring the Ideas

Consequentialists argue that there is no difference between choosing to act (or not act) with the *intention* of bringing about a particular intended consequence and choosing to act (or not act) with a *likelihood* of the same outcome.

Anscombe argues against this, illustrating her point with the example of a man who is solely responsible for a child's support and who must choose between two courses of action. He must either commit some unrelated injustice (like siphoning public money for a corrupt politician) under the threat of imprisonment, or he can refuse to engage in corruption and therefore be imprisoned by the politician, making it impossible for him to pay child support. According to the consequentialist view, he must weigh the "evil" of intentionally withdrawing child support (for, in consequentialism, all foreseen consequences are intended) against the evil of intentionally carrying out the unjust act.

Even if the unjust act is evil, the consequentialists would say that the man is justified in choosing to do it because this way he does not stop supporting the child. Anscombe says this is a problem: "A man is responsible for the bad consequences of his bad actions, but gets no credit for the good ones; and contrariwise is not responsible for the bad consequences of good actions."[2]

Anscombe goes on to discuss what she describes as action intended "under a description." By this, she essentially means that an action that is not sufficiently described or explained can be misunderstood morally. For example, destroying someone's home would normally be considered unjust. However, if you destroyed the home in order to prevent a fire from leaping from one village to another, the circumstances would change how we regarded the action in moral terms.

Consequentialists would argue, however, that in such a case it is the *consequences* that make an act of injustice morally right (in this case, of course, saving the other houses). But for Anscombe, intention makes a crucial difference. She argues that the nuanced description of the action would mean that the consequentialists are incorrect to say that injustice is rendered moral by its expected consequences:[3] burning a house down in order to prevent a fire from spreading just cannot be accurately described either as "injustice" or as "arson."

As we have seen, David Hume made a distinction between "is" and "ought." Anscombe argues that many ordinary factual statements imply an obligation—an "ought," in other words, is already present in the "is." If I owe someone money, I "ought" to pay the debt. So, if the butcher has delivered some meat to me, I owe money and ought to pay it. In other words, an analysis of justice shows that we *could* derive an "ought" from an "is." A statement of facts about relationships and institutions will contain the information necessary to decide on a just course of action.

Finally, Anscombe revives rich concepts based on virtue ethics—like justice and callousness—to replace "ought" and "right." For instance, choosing an abortion because you would no longer be able to afford to go on international holidays if you had a child would be an example of the vice of callousness, whereas choosing an abortion to save the life of the mother should not be called callous, regardless of any other ethical considerations.[4] Here she is in direct confrontation with the consequentialists, for whom any act might be permissible even if it is callous, provided it leads to the best foreseeable consequences.

Overlooked

As a very famous and relatively concise paper, "Modern Moral Philosophy" has been thoroughly examined, criticized, and interpreted. There is, though, one fairly brief comment in it that could be explored further.

Anscombe argues against Immanuel Kant's* approach to moral philosophy, dismissing it on the basis that it requires the concept of "legislating for oneself,"[5] which she considers nonsensical. When she was writing, Wittgenstein's* analysis of rule-following and of non-referential language use was a hot topic at Oxford and

Cambridge universities, as was philosophy in "ordinary language"; Anscombe could assume a familiarity with these ideas. Kantian ethics,* however, had few followers.

Since then a new interest in Kant's ethics has emerged. The American virtue ethicist John Rawls's* influential *A Theory of Justice* (1971),[6] for instance, has brought Kant into the foreground again and so given Anscombe's arguments against him a wider audience. One scholar devotes an entire chapter to the legalistic conception of morality in his book on Anscombe's philosophy.[7] Anscombe herself wrote a further paper, "Rules, Rights and Promises,"[8] which develops the idea of the nature of obligation and committing oneself to a rule.

NOTES

1   G. E. M. Anscombe, "Modern Moral Philosophy," *Philosophy* 33, no. 124 (1958): 9.

2   Anscombe, "Modern Moral Philosophy," 10.

3   Anscombe "Modern Moral Philosophy," 13.

4   For a later development of this idea, see Rosalind Hursthouse, "Virtue Theory and Abortion," *Philosophy and Public Affairs* 20, no. 3 (1999): 238–42.

5   Anscombe "Modern Moral Philosophy," 2.

6   John Rawls, *A Theory of Justice* (Cambridge, MA: Harvard University Press, 1971).

7   Roger Teichmann, *The Philosophy of Elizabeth Anscombe* (Oxford: Oxford University Press, 2008).

8   G. E. M. Anscombe, "Rules, Rights and Promises," in *Ethics, Religion and Politics* (Oxford: Basil Blackwell, 1981).

ACHIEVEMENT

KEY POINTS

- Anscombe challenged consequentialism* and initiated a new program in moral philosophy: virtue ethics.*

- Virtue ethics has useful applications in government policy and medical ethics.*

- Anscombe's Christianity may have limited the paper's impact; some have dismissed it as an implicit argument for belief in God.

Assessing the Argument

In "Modern Moral Philosophy," G. E. M. Anscombe set out to reform her entire field of study. Her aims were threefold: to demonstrate that moral philosophy cannot be carried out "until we have an adequate philosophy of psychology, in which we are conspicuously lacking";[1] to show the problems inherent in "moral obligation"* and "ought" without belief in a divine legislator for morality; and to demonstrate that most English moral philosophers of the previous 75 years were ultimately the same— they all rejected Christianity and accepted consequentialism.

The essay was ambitious, but it did at least partially meet her aims. She succeeded in making a stinging criticism of consequentialism and Kantian ethics* on conceptual and moral grounds. The impact was immediate and many moral philosophers turned away from consequentialism.[2] She also raised enough contrasts between Aristotle's* moral philosophy and modern moral philosophy to revive an interest in virtue ethics. Anscombe's arguments in favor of the virtues were framed in an extremely engaging and interesting way, and this inspired other philosophers to follow her lead.

> ❝ "Modern Moral Philosophy"initiated the return to the idea of virtues as the central concepts needed by moral thought. It was enormously influential, turning firstly most of her Oxford generation, and then probably a majority of philosophers worldwide, against utilitarianism as a moral and political theory. ❞
>
> Simon Blackburn "Against Anscombe," *Times Literary Supplement*

Achievement in Context

Although Anscombe's "Modern Moral Philosophy" is primarily a philosophical text, it was also directly relevant to the political and social trends of the day. World War II* had seen virtually indiscriminate bombing of cities such as Dresden, Germany, resulting in huge civilian casualties on both sides. This had raised new moral questions because this mentality of "total war" meant that states justified the killing of civilians as a means of ending the war. Anscombe was appalled by this and it led to her questioning how such immoral thinking had come about. Her conclusion was that all the English moral philosophers from the Victorian philosopher Henry Sidgwick* to her day offered a justification. So Anscombe's arguments—that actions like intentionally killing innocent civilians can never be countenanced, whatever the supposed benefits—were radical in her day. As a result, some saw Anscombe as holding an extreme moral position.[3]

Anscombe was something of a revolutionary, given that she was one of the first philosophers in generations to propose that moral philosophy should return to virtue ethics. This meant that her essay was undervalued initially. However, because her thinking was so different from that of other moral philosophers of the time, her ideas had the benefit of novelty and gradually gathered support.

Limitations

A possible limitation of "Modern Moral Philosophy" is that it focused on Anscombe's contemporaries and their approach to moral philosophy. These included the philosophers R. M. Hare* and Patrick Nowell-Smith.* She essentially charges them with being unoriginal, stating that the differences between them and their predecessors are "of little importance."[4] While Anscombe was mainly challenging philosophers who are today mostly forgotten, she also included several important moral philosophers across the history of philosophy.

As a result, even if the argument about the similarity between consequentialist* philosophers seems dated, two other elements in the essay have a universal application. The first is the general analysis of the concept of morality and the relationship between moral obligation and a presumed divine legislative force. The second is the contrast between consequentialist approaches to ethics and virtue-based approaches.

One difficulty readers have found with Anscombe's essay is its ambiguity about the relationship between religion and moral philosophy. Some philosophers have interpreted Anscombe as asserting that atheists cannot meaningfully use moral concepts and, as a result, have taken offence and largely ignored the essay. The British philosopher Simon Blackburn,* for instance, wrote: "If I feel I must avoid [words like "ought" and "obligation"] because I have been told that they are the private preserve of people who believe in divine law, then I have been hoodwinked and robbed."[5]

Most commentators, however, disagree with Blackburn. Anscombe scholars mostly claim that far from arguing against the possibility of secular moral philosophy, she wanted to help secular philosophers develop a conceptual framework for moral philosophy based on the virtues rather than on theological concepts.

NOTES

1   G. E. M. Anscombe, "Modern Moral Philosophy," *Philosophy* 33, no. 124 (1958): 1.

2   Simon Blackburn, "Against Anscombe: Review of *Human Life, Action and Ethics*," *Times Literary Supplement*, September 30, 2005: 11–12.

3   This is reflected in the fact that only four other academics at Oxford University voted no to the awarding of an honorary doctorate to US president Harry S. Truman—the only world leader to have used the atomic bomb on human beings.

4   Anscombe, "Modern Moral Philosophy," 1.

5   Simon Blackburn, "Review of *Human Life, Action and Ethics*."

PLACE IN THE AUTHOR'S WORK

KEY POINTS

- Anscombe's writing was eclectic. She translated Wittgenstein's* *Philosophical Investigations*,[1] wrote *Intention*[2] (a seminal work in action theory),* and initiated the field of virtue ethics* with her paper "Modern Moral Philosophy."

- "Modern Moral Philosophy" is perhaps rivaled only by her book Intention in terms of its influence.

- Although many know her principally as Wittgenstein's translator, "Modern Moral Philosophy" marks Anscombe out as a philosopher in her own right.

Positioning

G. E. M. Anscombe's "Modern Moral Philosophy" was published in 1958, when she was at the height of her philosophical career. She had already published papers on varied topics and enjoyed a prominent position in British philosophy. Anscombe had made a very important translation of Wittgenstein's posthumously published *Philosophical Investigations* in 1953, and Wittgenstein remained perhaps the main influence on her thinking. Anscombe's work in moral philosophy was essentially begun in earnest, however, in 1957–8.

In 1957, Anscombe gave the radio address "Does Oxford Moral Philosophy Corrupt the Youth?", in which she criticized the way that moral philosophy was taught at Oxford University. The following year, "Modern Moral Philosophy" was her philosophical response to the perceived incoherence of contemporary moral systems.

> **"** Elizabeth Anscombe was widely recognized as the most brilliant of Wittgenstein's students, as well as the pre-eminent translator and interpreter of his works. She was also an original and formidable philosopher in her own right, apparently able to reconcile a staunch Roman Catholicism with what she had learned from Frege, Aristotle, or Wittgenstein himself. **"**
>
> Simon Blackburn "Against Anscombe," *Times Literary Supplement*

Also in 1958 Anscombe published an important pamphlet, "Mr. Truman's Degree,"[3] which criticized both US President Harry S. Truman* for his bombing of civilians in the Japanese cities of Hiroshima and Nagasaki,* and Oxford University for subsequently honoring him with a degree. In fact, several of Anscombe's publications were connected in some way with World War II and its aftermath. Her very first publication—*The Justice of the Present War Examined*[4]—was written in 1939 on the subject of the morality of World War II. It is no overstatement to say that the policies of the Allies (the forces led by the United States and Britain) during World War II, bombing civilian targets, demanding unconditional surrender, and so on, were the most significant cause for Anscombe's reflection on moral philosophy. Her 1971 lecture "Causality and Determination"[5] was also a philosophically influential work.

Integration

Anscombe's life's work focused on the analysis of human action. She explored in technical detail what it was to "intend" to do something, writing *Intention* on this subject in 1957. This book, still considered one of the classics of twentieth-century philosophy, has been cited well over 3,000 times in scholarly articles and books.

"Modern Moral Philosophy" fits within Anscombe's broader research examining the philosophy of how we *ought* to act—the question of moral obligation* (a requirement upon an individual to do something or refrain from doing something).

Anscombe's writings in the area of Roman Catholic* Christian morality cannot be ignored. Her works "Contraception and Chastity"[6] and "Action, Intention and 'Double Effect'"[7] have been influential both among Catholics and others. However, there is no real boundary between Anscombe's Catholic-informed ideas and her moral philosophy. For example, she shows her dismay at the contemporary loss of belief in natural moral law in "The Justice of the Present War Examined"—a work of Catholic moral theology. This idea was clearly a precursor to her argument in "Modern Moral Philosophy" that moral obligation had been stripped of its meaningful content by the rejection of Christianity.

Significance

The paper "Modern Moral Philosophy" is Anscombe's most influential work of moral philosophy. Perhaps only her book *Intention* can be said to have similar importance. The latter was published earlier and first brought Anscombe to prominence as a thinker.

One of the most important works in moral philosophy of the twentieth century, Anscombe's paper makes contributions in two principal areas. First, it initiated the virtue ethics movement in moral philosophy. Virtue ethics emphasizes qualities of character—like justice, courage, and wisdom—and their impact upon specific actions. The movement has included influential moral philosophers like Philippa Foot,* Alasdair MacIntyre,* and Rosalind Hursthouse.* Virtue ethics has gradually grown in prominence and nowadays enjoys widespread popularity among moral philosophers. An entire anthology was devoted to the virtue ethics movement in 2013—something that scholars trace back to Anscombe's article.[8] As the British moral philosopher Anthony O'Hear* summarizes: "In some quarters and in some ways, moral philosophy was changed by Anscombe's article and, in the opinion of many, for the better."[9]

Second, Anscombe's essay created significant interest in the question of moral obligation and divine command ethics.* Like Anscombe, divine command theorists maintain that there is a link between God and moral obligation. This view has been defended by the American philosophers Philip L. Quinn,* in *Divine Commands and Moral Requirements*,[10] and Robert Adams,* in *Finite and Infinite Goods*.[11] Adams has been influential, arguing that "obligation," "guilt," and "moral ought" are intrinsically social and therefore do require a divine being to whom we are accountable. This approach is very much in agreement with "Modern Moral Philosophy," as the social nature of these concepts can be accounted for by God.

NOTES

1   Ludwig Wittgenstein, *Philosophical Investigations (Philosophische Untersuchungen) Eng. & Ger*, trans. G. E. M. Anscombe (Oxford: Basil Blackwell, 1953).

2   G. E. M. Anscombe, *Intention* (Oxford: Oxford University Press, 1957).

3   G. E. M. Anscombe, "Mr. Truman's Degree," in *Ethics, Religion and Politics* (Oxford: Basil Blackwell, 1981).

4   G. E. M. Anscombe, "The Justice of the Present War Examined," in *Ethics, Religion and Politics* (London: Basil Blackwell, 1981).

5   G. E. M. Anscombe, *Causality and Determination: An Inaugural Lecture* (Cambridge: Cambridge University Press, 1971).

6   G. E. M. Anscombe, *Contraception and Chastity* (London: Catholic Truth Society, 1975).

7   G. E. M. Anscombe, "Action, Intention and 'Double-Effect'," *Proceedings of the American Catholic Philosophical Association* 56 (1982): 12–25.

8   Daniel C. Russell, ed., *The Cambridge Companion to Virtue Ethics* (Cambridge: Cambridge University Press, 2013), 5.

9   Anthony O'Hear, "Preface," *Modern Moral Philosophy: Royal Institute of Philosophy Supplement 54*, ed. Anthony O'Hear (Cambridge: Cambridge University Press, 2004).

10 See Philip Quinn, *Divine Commands and Moral Requirements* (Oxford: Clarendon Library of Logic and Philosophy, 1978).

11 Robert Adams, *Finite and Infinite Goods: A Framework for Ethics* (Oxford: Oxford University Press, 2002).

SECTION 3
IMPACT

MODULE 9
THE FIRST RESPONSES

KEY POINTS

- Critics of "Modern Moral Philosophy" argue that moral obligation* is possible without divine authority, that there are defenses to her critique of consequentialism,* and that virtue ethics* needs to be explored further.

- Anscombe and her followers have maintained that distinguishing between foreseen and intended consequences is vital for clarity in moral philosophy; and that since virtue ethics does not rely on divine authority, it is a plausible ethical philosophy.

- Anscombe went on to develop a more nuanced view of the relationship between human actions and their foreseen consequences.

Criticism

One of the most widespread criticisms of G. E. M. Anscombe's "Modern Moral Philosophy" was that she had failed to argue persuasively the case that morality depended on a belief in God.

The philosopher Kai Nielsen,* for example, wrote an article criticizing Anscombe called "Some Remarks on the Independence of Morality From Religion."[1] He states, "No … knowledge that there is a God and that He issues commands, will by itself tell us what is good or what we ought to do."[2] This problem had been raised by the ancient Greek philosopher Plato in his work *Euthyphro*,[3] and is summarized in the so-called *Euthyphro* dilemma: does God's command make an action right, or does God command certain actions because those actions are themselves already right? If

> **❝** No ... knowledge that there is a God and that He issues commands, will by itself tell us what is good or what we ought to do. **❞**
>
> Kai Nielsen, "Some Remarks on the Independence of Morality from Religion"

the former is the case, then God could command heinous acts. If the latter, then God is not the basis of morality after all. Nielsen asserted that this question had been settled "since the *Euthyphro*."[4]

Another criticism came from consequentialists who set out to defend their moral theory. One example was the American philosopher Jonathan Bennett,* who argued that Anscombe's distinction between intended and merely foreseen consequences was morally irrelevant. Using examples from medical ethics, Bennett argued there is in fact no morally relevant difference between killing and allowing to die.[5] For example, a physician who stands by while someone goes into cardiac arrest cannot be excused for having simply "let the person die" rather than having "killed" the person. Positive reviews of Anscombe's work focused particularly on the revival of the virtues in moral philosophy.

Responses

Unfortunately, Anscombe did not respond to the charge that she had argued unpersuasively for the dependence of morality upon religion. There is in fact some contention among commentators as to whether she intended the paper to imply an argument for belief in God. While some continue to assert that she did,[6] the consensus view seems to be that it was not her primary intention to make such an argument—though that, of course, does not mean that she did not believe in such a link. The philosopher D. J. Richter* argues: "It is a mistake to conclude from [Anscombe's] argument that only a divine law or Aristotelian conception of ethics will do," because Anscombe herself explores such alternatives and finds them insufficient.[7] In short, Anscombe is open to other accounts of moral obligation; she just finds all of those accounts grossly lacking.

Anscombe's clearest response to criticism of "Modern Moral Philosophy" came in a very short note in the journal *Analysis* in response to Bennett's criticism of her distinction between acts and consequences.[8] She writes: "The nerve of Mr. Bennett's argument is that if A results from your not doing B, then A results from whatever you do instead of doing B. While there may be much to be said for this view, still it does not seem right on the face of it."[9] This exchange came at the very beginning of Anscombe's work on the relevance of intention to any philosophy of morality.

Conflict and Consensus

Although Anscombe seems to have held to her criticism of consequentialism to the last, she did seek to develop greater conceptual clarity about how to judge the morality of actions with bad foreseen but unintended consequences. Indeed, her talk "Action, Intention and 'Double-Effect'"[10] is a highly developed account of these concepts. Anscombe argues that if you foresee that deaths will almost certainly occur as a result of building a highway, you cannot reasonably be said to "intend" that foreseen consequence—and so you cannot be said to be guilty. She seems to have been spurred on to answer the criticisms of consequentialists like Bennett, who rejected her distinction between intended and foreseen consequences. He and others had done so on the basis of the charge that Anscombe was merely rehearsing the Roman Catholic* doctrine of double-effect: that you may not kill a person as a means to other (even good) ends, but that you may carry out an action that has the expected side effect of causing someone's death.

Anscombe responds in "Action, Intention, and 'Double-Effect'" that she is not a defender of "double-effect" but of the "principle of side-effects," writing: "'The principle of side-effects' is related to an absolute prohibition on seeking someone's death, either as an end or as means … It does not say when you may foreseeably cause death."[11] In short, Anscombe is interested *only* in showing that it is not always wrong to do something with the certain knowledge that someone's death will directly result. Her principle is meant to demonstrate what is different about the case of transplanting an organ from a living person and building a high-speed highway. They both result in the foreseen consequence of at least one person's death—but for her, the first is murder and the second is not.

NOTES

1   Kai Nielsen, "Some Remarks on the Independence of Morality From Religion," *Mind* 70, no. 278 (1961): 175–86.

2   Nielsen, "Some Remarks," 175.

3   See Plato, *Euthyphro*, in *Readings in Ancient Greek Philosophy*, 2nd edition, ed. S. Marc Cohen and Patricia Curd, trans. C. D. C. Reeve (Indianapolis: Hackett Publishing, 2005), 97–114.

4   Nielsen, "Some Remarks," 175.

5   Jonathan Bennett, "Whatever the Consequences," *Analysis* 26, no. 2 (1966), 83–102.

6   See Thomas Pink, "Moral Obligation," in *Modern Moral Philosophy: Royal Institute of Philosophy Supplement 54*, ed. Anthony O'Hear (Cambridge: Cambridge University Press, 2004), 159–69; and Nielsen, "Some Remarks."

7   D. J. Richter, *Ethics after Anscombe: Post "Modern Moral Philosophy"* (Dordrecht: Springer Publishers, 2000), 29.

8   Bennett, "Whatever the Consequences."

9   G. E. M. Anscombe, "A Note on Mr. Bennett," *Analysis* 26, no. 6 (1966): 208.

10 G. E. M. Anscombe, "Action, Intention and 'Double-Effect,'" *Proceedings of the American Catholic Philosophical Association*, vol. 56 (1982): 12–25.

11 Anscombe, "Intention, Action and 'Double-Effect.'"

THE EVOLVING DEBATE

KEY POINTS

- Virtue ethics* is a flourishing topic in moral philosophy and has opened the way for alternatives to consequentialism.*

- Virtue ethics sees the purpose of moral philosophy as being the analysis of virtues such as wisdom and temperance using psychology, literature, and history.

- "Modern Moral Philosophy" introduced a new subfield of moral philosophy, which continues to develop in a great number of directions.

Uses and Problems

G. E. M. Anscombe's "Modern Moral Philosophy" raised deep problems with the concept of "moral obligation"* and "moral ought." According to Anscombe, "The concepts of obligation, and duty … ought to be jettisoned if this is psychologically possible."[1]

This idea did not appeal to those philosophers who followed Kantian ethics* and utilitarianism* (for whom Anscombe coined the term "consequentialists"). Both of these theories rely upon a secular account of "moral obligation" and Anscombe was questioning whether such a concept had any meaning.

As the philosopher Simon Blackburn* has since conceded, the text was "enormously influential, turning firstly most of her Oxford generation, and then probably a majority of philosophers worldwide, against utilitarianism as a moral and political theory."[2] As a result, a search began for an understanding of morality in the tradition of virtue ethics. Anscombe had ignited interest in virtue ethics generally and in the ethics of Aristotle* specifically.

> ❝ Elizabeth Anscombe's 'Modern Moral Philosophy' ... has played a significant part in the development of so-called 'virtue ethics,' which has burgeoned over the last three decades in particular. ❞
>
> Roger Crisp, "Does Modern Moral Philosophy Rest on a Mistake?"

Schools of Thought

This new approach to ethics has spawned a great deal of research in the fields of virtue ethics and experimental moral psychology. Although Anscombe herself did not pursue a full conceptual account of virtue ethics, her work encouraged many other philosophers to try to forge a way of using the virtues in contemporary moral philosophy.

Anscombe's close friend and fellow philosopher Philippa Foot* wrote *Virtues and Vices*[3] and *Natural Goodness*,[4] two classics in virtue ethics. Peter Geach,* Anscombe's husband, also wrote a book called *The Virtues* in 1974. Both Foot and Geach argue for a "naturalistic" account of the virtues—one grounded in human biology and sociology rather than "moral obligation." As Geach famously argued: "Men are benefited by virtues as bees are by having stings."[5] In other words, virtues are a normal part of the character of normal human beings; we are defective without them and cannot flourish. Philippa Foot argues in her 2001 book *Natural Goodness* that human biology can provide grounds for virtue ethics.[6]

In addition to the virtue ethics movement in moral philosophy, Anscombe's essay also impacted the field of Christian ethics, or moral theology ("theology" refers to the systematic study of religious concepts, usually conducted through the analysis of Scripture). The theologians Stanley Hauerwas* and William Frankena,* for instance, began developing Christian interpretations of the virtues in the 1970s. Hauerwas's work, in particular, has assimilated the use of virtue ethics in Christian theology and life.[7]

In Current Scholarship

The contemporary virtue ethics movement is perhaps at the most prolific moment in its history; in 2013, Cambridge University Press produced an entire anthology devoted to virtue ethics.[8] One cannot overstate Anscombe's impact, and many questions addressed in the current movement can be traced back to her writings on the medieval* and ancient* proponents of virtue ethics.

Anscombe's comments on the ethics of Aristotle and the medieval theologian Thomas Aquinas* were significant contributions. One of the most important figures in contemporary virtue ethics is Alasdair MacIntyre,* whose book *After Virtue* was published in 1981.[9] In it, MacIntyre takes up several of Anscombe's themes, including a detailed conceptual account of the virtues.[10] MacIntyre is also author of *Dependent Rational Animals*, which analyzes the impact of human biology on the way we should think about the virtues and moral development.[11]

Rosalind Hursthouse* of the University of Auckland is another leading figure in virtue ethics; she made a vital contribution to virtue ethics with her 2001 book *On Virtue Ethics*. Hursthouse argues that virtue ethics can produce what she calls "v-rules": rules centered on virtues and vices.[12] So if one comes to understand that having an abortion to further one's career would be a callous act, it follows that one ought not to have an abortion. These rules make virtue ethics a "normative" moral theory and therefore a rival to consequentialism and Kantian ethics.

The most recent proponents of virtue ethics are Martha Nussbaum* and the notable Indian economist Amartya Sen.* Martha Nussbaum is an American philosopher who specializes in ancient philosophy and literature. She produced several important works in moral psychology that emphasized the importance of emotions such as love, compassion, grief, shame, and disgust in ethical thinking. She also worked with Amartya Sen to develop the "capabilities" approach to welfare economics, focusing on the capabilities central to living a flourishing life. Nussbaum listed 10, including the capacity to form emotional attachments, to reason, to play, and to be healthy. This approach has been useful in comparing and measuring international development, and was instrumental in forming the Human Development Index—an international measure for developmental welfare.

NOTES

1   G. E. M. Anscombe, "Modern Moral Philosophy," *Philosophy* 33, no. 124 (1958): 1.

2   Simon Blackburn, "Against Anscombe: Review of *Human Life, Action and Ethics*," *Times Literary Supplement*, September 30, 2005: 11–12.

3   Philippa Foot, *Virtues and Vices and Other Essays in Moral Philosophy* (Berkeley and Los Angeles: University of California Press, 1978).

4   Philippa Foot, *Natural Goodness* (Oxford: Oxford University Press, 2001).

5   Peter Geach, *The Virtues* (Cambridge: Cambridge University Press, 1977), vii.

6   Foot, *Natural Goodness*, 51.

7   Stanley Hauerwas, *Character and the Christian Life* (San Antonio, TX: Trinity University Press, 1975).

8   Daniel C. Russell, ed., *The Cambridge Companion to Virtue Ethics* (Cambridge: Cambridge University Press, 2013).

9   Alasdair MacIntyre, *After Virtue*, 3rd revised edition (London: Duckworth, 2007).

10 MacIntyre, *After Virtue*, 191.

11 Alasdair MacIntyre, *Dependent Rational Animals* (London: Duckworth, 1999).

12 Rosalind Hursthouse, *On Virtue Ethics* (Oxford: Oxford University Press, 2001), 36–42.

IMPACT AND INFLUENCE TODAY

KEY POINTS

- "Modern Moral Philosophy" helps to define moral philosophy by dividing it into consequentialism,* Kantian ethics,* and virtue ethics.*

- It still poses the problem for Kantian ethics that Kant's* concept of legislating for oneself—passing and enforcing one's own "laws"—is incoherent.

- Anscombe targeted consequentialist and Kantian ethics as immoral.

Position

One significant contribution that G. E. M. Anscombe's "Modern Moral Philosophy" made to the contemporary debate is her coining of the term "consequentialism." Until her paper, a host of moral theories had been grouped under the term "utilitarianism"* (a moral and political philosophy that judges an action according to its capacity to cause the greatest happiness for the greatest number).

Her second main contribution was the raising of huge questions about moral obligation* (a requirement of an individual to do something or refrain from doing something); this has invited further research, including questioning whether ethics should be understood in "naturalist" or "nonnaturalist" terms. Those who argue for naturalist ethics believe there is an essential similarity between ethical judgments and everyday value judgments: if the farmer produces good vegetables and sustains his land, then he is a good farmer. Nonnaturalists argue that there is a gap between facts and values, so that the property of "goodness" or "rightness" must be a nonnatural property of certain

> ❝ Philosophers like Elizabeth Anscombe and Philippa Foot ... advocated a turn to virtue ethics as the logical conclusion of the contemporary quest to clarify and ground the central concepts of ethics. ❞
>
> Daniel C. Russell, *The Cambridge Companion to Virtue Ethics*

actions. For instance, it does not follow from the fact that football brings pleasure (according to nonnaturalists) that watching football is morally right. The pleasure that you experience must have the additional property of "goodness."

Finally, the essay divided the contemporary field of ethics into three main categories: consequentialism, Kantian ethics, and virtue ethics. Indeed, the paper is still regularly cited in a huge number of books and articles published on virtue ethics, and is therefore a key starting point for any student seeking to understand moral philosophy.

Interaction

"Modern Moral Philosophy" remains important today as the first major objection to consequentialism with enough depth to be able to initiate an alternative. Although the essay had a number of impacts on consequentialism, three stand out.

First, Anscombe argued that consequentialism implies that no kind of action is ruled out absolutely. Since it is at least possible that convicting and killing the innocent could have beneficial consequences, for example, a consequentialist can never simply prohibit such an injustice.

Second, Anscombe persuasively argued that although consequentialism, especially in its utilitarian forms, was entirely based on the concept of "pleasure," it cannot even give a full account of what pleasure is. As a result, consequentialists today often focus instead on the satisfaction of preferences, rather than the realization of pleasure.

Third, there remains considerable debate about the distinction between intended and merely foreseen consequences. Anscombe wrote on this subject again in "Action, Intention and 'Double-Effect'" in 1981, when she presented a detailed defense of the importance of distinguishing intended from foreseen consequences.[1] Many consequentialists, however, have maintained that there is not a morally significant difference between the two. The philosophy professor Jonathan Bennett, an early critic of Anscombe, explores the distinction further in "Morality and Consequences"[2] and *The Act Itself* (1995).[3]

The Continuing Debate

Anscombe argued against consequentialists "from Sidgwick to the present day."[4] One modern defender of consequentialism is the Australian philosopher Peter Singer,* who systematically defends Sidgwick in *The Point of View of the Universe: Sidgwick and Contemporary Ethics*.[5] The continued relevance of Sidgwick—for even the most prominent consequentialist philosophers like Singer—demonstrates the insight of Anscombe's claim that the publication of Sidgwick's *Methods of Ethics* (1874) was a watershed in the history of ethics.[6]

Unlike previous moral philosophers, Sidgwick and his followers deny that any kind of action is ruled out categorically. So, to take one of Peter Singer's favorite examples, killing an infant is not prohibited—provided that the infant is disabled and his parents want him killed. This is because, according to Singer, infants do not possess rational self-awareness, or personhood. He concludes in his book *Practical Ethics* that, therefore, "Reasons for not killing persons do not apply to newborn infants."[7] Anscombe's moral arguments become particularly relevant here as current consequentialists consider an act as heinous as infanticide in terms of a mere cost–benefit analysis.

Anscombe also targets Kantian ethics in her paper. The Kantian approach has seen a major upturn since the publication of "Modern

Moral Philosophy." Perhaps the foremost Kantian moral philosopher is Christine Korsgaard* of Harvard University, whose 1996 book *The Sources of Normativity* is a systematic defense of his position. Although Anscombe said that the idea that one can legislate for oneself is absurd, Korsgaard argues that self-reflection gives humans the possibility of becoming their own moral authorities.[8] Since "authority" is normally the province of a greater power over a lesser, however, it is unclear exactly how Korsgaard's account overturns Anscombe's argument in "Modern Moral Philosophy."

NOTES

1   G. E. M. Anscombe, *Human Life, Action and Ethics*, ed. by Mary Geach and Luke Gormally (Exeter: Imprint Academic, 2005), Kindle edition.

2   Jonathan Bennett, "Morality and Consequences," in *The Tanner Lectures on Human Values*, vol. 2, ed. by Sterling McMurrin (Salt Lake City: University of Utah Press, 1981), 110–11.

3   Jonathan Bennett, *The Act Itself* (New York: Oxford University Press, 1995), 194–225.

4   G. E. M. Anscombe, "Modern Moral Philosophy," *Philosophy* 33, no. 124 (1958): 1.

5   Katarzyna de Lazari-Radek and Peter Singer, *The Point of View of the Universe: Sidgwick and Contemporary Ethics* (Oxford: Oxford University Press, 2014).

6   Henry Sidgwick, *Methods of Ethics*, 7th edition (Indianapolis: Hackett, 1981).

7   Peter Singer, *Practical Ethics* (Cambridge: Cambridge University Press, 1979), 124.

8   Christine Korsgaard, *The Sources of Normativity* (Cambridge: Cambridge University Press, 1996), 19–20.

WHERE NEXT?

KEY POINTS

- "Modern Moral Philosophy" will continue to be an important text because it provides both strong arguments and an alternative to consequentialism* and Kantian ethics.*

- The essay reinvigorated virtue ethics* as an approach to moral philosophy.

- Research on virtue ethics will continue to expand in fruitful directions in the future.

Potential

Having helped transform moral philosophy in the twentieth and twenty-first centuries, G. E. M. Anscombe's "Modern Moral Philosophy" will remain an influential text. The essay continues to provide a clear and well-argued critique of consequentialist and Kantian moral philosophy. It will continue to be a standard essay for philosophy students because it raises deep questions about the nature of moral obligation,* it contrasts the theories of some of the most influential moral thinkers in the history of philosophy, and its publication was a watershed moment in the history of the virtue ethics tradition in moral philosophy.

The greatest potential for the text in the future lies in its capacity to inspire philosophers to pursue enquiry into virtue ethics. There are indications that virtue ethics, while remaining a minority view, will continue to rise in popularity and academic rigor. Specifically, virtue ethics is beginning to be appropriated in areas like applied ethics* (the subfield of moral philosophy that focuses on applying moral principles to concrete situations) and its subfield of bioethics*

> **❝In some quarters and in some ways, moral philosophy was changed by Anscombe's article and, in the opinion of many, for the better. ❞**
> Anthony O'Hear, *Modern Moral Philosophy*

(which inquires into medical and environmental ethical issues) and to political philosophy. The year 2013 saw the publication of an anthology of "applied virtue ethics" called *Virtues in Action: New Essays in Applied Virtue Ethics*,[1] for example. Topics cover a range of issues including "The Virtues of Honourable Business Executives" and "Humility and Environmental Virtue Ethics."

Similarly, the *Cambridge Companion to Virtue Ethics*[2] was published for the first time in 2013—as were dozens of articles and books on the subject of the virtues.

Future Directions

Although "Modern Moral Philosophy" lays out a new direction for moral philosophy, certain aspects need to be developed—among them a philosophical analysis of moral psychology, accounts of the virtues, and an understanding of "above all, human flourishing."[3] These themes continue to be developed in fascinating directions. The American philosopher Martha Nussbaum,* for instance, is a contemporary virtue ethicist who writes about human flourishing. She has produced several important works on moral psychology that emphasize the importance of such emotions as love, compassion, grief, shame, and disgust in ethical thinking. She worked with Amartya Sen,* winner of the Nobel Prize in economics in 1998, to develop the "capabilities" approach to welfare economics that defines welfare in terms of the capabilities central to living a flourishing life.

Nussbaum listed, among others, the capability to form emotional attachments, to reason, to play, and to be healthy as essential capabilities. The capabilities approach has been useful in comparing and measuring international development and was instrumental in forming the Human Development Index, an international measure for developmental welfare. Perhaps this direction of the virtue ethics movement—human flourishing and human virtues in relation to politics and economics—will prove one of the most fruitful.

Summary

"Modern Moral Philosophy" remains one of the most important texts in twentieth-century moral philosophy. In it, G. E. M. Anscombe's keen analytical eye ranges over consequentialism, Kantian ethics, and contractualism,* and finds each of them either immoral or conceptually incoherent.

Consequentialism depends upon a questionable concept of "pleasure," she finds, and leads to immoral conclusions (consequentialists must be open, for example, to the possibility that condemning the innocent to death is the "right" thing to do—provided it has some positive consequence overall). This view, says Anscombe, is characteristic of someone who "has a corrupt mind."[4] Kantian ethics depends upon the concept of legislating for oneself, which she finds incoherent. Contractualism makes morality dependent on whatever the majority happens to believe at any one time, which again leads to disastrous moral conclusions.

Additionally, Anscombe raises questions about the nature of "moral" words like "obligation," "ought," and "right," and argues that the concepts as used by contemporary philosophers do not make sense as they have no belief in a divine lawmaker. This is because the concepts are intrinsically social ones—you are commanded to do something or prohibited from doing something by a greater power. However, Anscombe pushes her readers to seek an alternative way of discussing good and bad human action. This method, she argues, will depend upon richer concepts, like "justice," "virtue," and "charity." This resulted in the development of the virtue ethics movement, which has become influential in moral philosophy over the past 40 years.

These aspects make "Modern Moral Philosophy" one of the most important essays in the history of moral philosophy. Every reader will benefit from the questions and arguments Anscombe raises in a work that provides a wonderful introduction to those wishing to understand the state of moral philosophy from the middle of the twentieth century to the present day.

NOTES

1   Michael W. Austin, ed., *Virtues in Action: New Essays in Applied Virtue Ethics* (Basingstoke: Palgrave Macmillan, 2013).

2   Daniel C. Russell, ed., *The Cambridge Companion to Virtue Ethics* (Cambridge: Cambridge University Press, 2013).

3   G. E. M. Anscombe, "Modern Moral Philosophy," *Philosophy* 33, no. 124 (1958): 1–16.

4   Anscombe, "Modern Moral Philosophy," 14.

GLOSSARIES

GLOSSARY OF TERMS

Action theory: a subfield of philosophy that analyzes the nature of human action. It involves questions about the mind, determinism, and free will.

Analytic philosophy: a philosophical set of methods that focuses on detailed analysis of concepts and language. It is the dominant method in Britain and the United States, and its roots were in late nineteenth- and early twentieth-century philosophy at the University of Cambridge.

Ancient: in philosophy, the period of ancient Greek and Roman philosophy was from roughly 400 B.C.E. to 200 C.E. Important figures include Plato, Aristotle, and Cicero.

Applied ethics: the subfield of moral philosophy that focuses on applying moral principles to concrete situations. It contains further subdivisions such as "bioethics" and the ethics of technology.

Aristotelian approach to ethics: a version of ethical theory that draws substantially from the ancient Greek philosopher Aristotle. Aristotle based ethics on the virtues, as well as the concept of *eudaimonia* (roughly, happiness).

Bioethics: a subfield of moral philosophy that focuses on medical ethics, ethics of the environment, and ethics of animal treatment. It was developed largely in the 1960s.

Bombing of Hiroshima and Nagasaki: in 1945, the United States—under the authority of President Harry S. Truman—bombed the major Japanese cities of Hiroshima and Nagasaki in order to bring an end to World War II. The act remains controversial and is considered by many an act of mass murder of civilians.

Categorical imperative: the imperative that applies in all cases; the theory that one should always act in accordance with maxims that one can choose as a universal law.

Consequentialism: a term coined by Anscombe in "Modern Moral Philosophy" that now has broad currency. It refers to any moral philosophy that defines the moral value of an action solely in terms of its consequences.

Contractualism: a theory of morality that proposes that an implicit contract exists between members of a community and that this contract grounds moral obligation.

Deontology: a moral philosophy focusing on duties. Kant's ethical philosophy is the prime example; this argues that every rational being has the duty to obey the categorical imperative.

Determinism: the philosophical view that every event in the universe (including every human action) is causally determined by the previous state of the physical universe.

Divine command ethics/Divine law ethics: a theory of moral obligation that asserts that actions are obligatory which have the property of being commanded by God.

Ethical anti-realism: the thesis that moral facts do not exist. While consequentialism is the thesis that consequences alone have moral value, one can arguably be a consequentialist and be either an ethical anti-realist or a realist.

Ethical intuitionism: the view that individuals know moral truths because they have direct access to moral facts through a faculty of intuition. It was developed by the philosophers Henry Sidgwick and G. E. Moore.

Ethics: the subdiscipline of philosophy that focuses on the theoretical and practical aspects of morality. It seeks primarily to answer the questions "What is the nature of the good life?" and "How ought we to live?"

Kantian ethics: a theory of moral obligation (sometimes called "deontology") that asserts that one's obligation is to act in ways one would at the same time prescribe as a universal moral law.

Law conception of ethics: any conception of ethics that uses legalistic language such as "obligation," "ought," "right," and "permitted." This conception of ethics has its roots in early Christian belief in divine law authorized by God.

Medical ethics: a subfield of applied ethics that focuses on the ethics of medicine. Central themes include patient and physician autonomy, abortion, euthanasia, and medical testing on human subjects.

Medieval: The medieval period of philosophy was roughly from 400 to 1400 c.e. In the West, it was characterized most importantly by Christian philosophical and theological reflection.

Meta-ethics: a philosophy concerned with the nature of ethical propositions and the foundations of morality.

Metaphysics: the study of the ultimate nature of reality.

Moral obligation: refers in philosophy to a requirement upon an individual to do something or refrain from doing something. A moral obligation is normally believed to override other requirements—either self-interest or social expectations.

Moral philosophy: another term for ethics.

Naturalistic fallacy: a concept developed by the philosopher G. E. Moore. Moore argued that, for any natural property of a thing, one could question whether that property was good or bad; therefore to identify goodness itself with such a property is a mistake.

Normativity: the area of philosophy that focuses on norms, or action-guiding rules, for behavior, emotions, or belief.

Progressivism: a social and political view that makes "progress" the highest political aim. It is linked with consequentialism in ethics.

Roman Catholicism: a form of Christianity that dates back to the lives of Jesus Christ's first followers. The world's largest Christian denomination, Roman Catholicism has a tradition of producing world-leading philosophers.

Utilitarianism: a moral and political philosophy that rates the best action to be the one that produces the greatest happiness in the greatest number. The theory's greatest advocates were social and legal reformers Jeremy Bentham and John Stuart Mill.

Verificationism: a view that asserts that propositions are meaningful only if they can in principle be verified by logic or empirical research. Verificationism's greatest advocate was British philosopher A. J. Ayer.

Victorian period: the time of Queen Victoria's reign in Great Britain: 1837–1901. It was characterized by British imperialism and industrialization.

Virtue ethics: an approach to normative ethics that identifies the good life in terms of attaining, and acting in accord with, virtues such as justice, wisdom, and generosity.

The virtues: dispositions of character that are expressed in human action. They include justice, temperance, and courage, and they form the core of the virtue ethics approach to moral philosophy.

World War II (1939–45): the single greatest armed conflict in human history, World War II engaged the Allies (for example, Great Britain, the United States, and the Soviet Union) against the Axis Powers (Nazi Germany, Italy, and Japan). It pushed forward one of the world's most rapid periods of modernization.

PEOPLE MENTIONED IN THE TEXT

Robert Adams (b. 1937) is an American philosopher who specializes in moral philosophy and metaphysics. Adams's most important contributions have been to the divine command theory of obligation, namely his *Finite and Infinite Goods* (1999).

Thomas Aquinas, also known as Tommaso d'Aquino (1225–74) was a particularly influential theologian, philosopher, and educator of the medieval period.

Aristotle (384–322 B.C.E.) was an ancient Greek philosopher who first coined the term "ethics." His ethical philosophy was based on perfecting the virtues by reaching the golden mean between extremes of behavior.

A. J. Ayer (1910–89) was an English philosopher known for verificationism and emotivism about ethics, which believes that ethical statements are not propositions, but expressions of emotion.

Jonathan Bennett (b. 1930) is professor emeritus in the philosophy department at Syracuse University. His specialisms are philosophy of mind and the history of philosophy.

Jeremy Bentham (1748–1832) was an English philosopher and social reformer regarded as the pioneer of the philosophical school of utilitarianism. He argued that an action's morality should be judged by how much pleasure it produced and how much pain it prevented or alleviated.

Simon Blackburn (b. 1944) is a prominent British philosopher and retired Bertrand Russell Professor of Philosophy at the University of Cambridge. His books, in the school of Hume's philosophy, include *Spreading the Word* (1984) and *Essays in Quasi-realism* (1993).

Philippa Foot (1920–2010) was an English philosopher whose work chiefly refocused professional ethical philosophical discussion around virtues and vices as opposed to consequences or duties.

William Frankena (1908–94) was an influential American philosopher who taught at the University of Michigan. His specialism was moral philosophy, and his most influential work was *Ethics* (1963).

Peter Geach (1916–2013) was an English philosopher who specialized in logic and moral philosophy. His most notable works are *The Virtues* (1977) and "Ascriptivism" (1960).

R. M. Hare (1919–2002) was a key English moral philosopher of the twentieth century. A utilitarian theorist, his most important work is *The Language of Morals* (1952).

Stanley Hauerwas (b. 1940) is a Christian ethicist and the Gilbert T. Rowe Professor Emeritus of Divinity at Duke University. His main works are *Character and the Christian Life* (1975) and *The Peaceable Kingdom* (1983).

David Hume (1711–76) was an influential Scottish empiricist philosopher who authored *Dialogues Concerning Natural Religion* (1779) and *An Enquiry Concerning the Principles of Morals* (1751). His moral theory sought to ground ethics in the human sentiments or feelings.

Rosalind Hursthouse (b. 1943) is professor of philosophy at the University of Auckland, New Zealand. She is a prominent neo-Aristotelian virtue ethicist, whose major works are "Virtue Theory and Abortion" (1991) and *On Virtue Ethics* (1999).

Immanuel Kant (1724–1804) was one of the most influential philosophers of the period of European intellectual history known as the Enlightenment (roughly 1750–1900, characterized by dramatic revolutions in the sciences and in philosophy, where increasing confidence was placed in the power of reason). He was the author of many works, including *Critique of Pure Reason* (1781) and *Groundwork of the Metaphysics of Morals* (1785), and he argued that ethics ought to be grounded in rationality.

Christine Korsgaard (b. 1952) is professor of philosophy at Harvard University. A Kantian moral philosopher, her most important work is *The Sources of Normativity* (1996).

Alasdair MacIntyre (b. 1929) is a Scottish moral philosopher who has held teaching positions at several major US universities. His most important works are in virtue ethics and include *After Virtue* (1981) and *Dependent Rational Animals: Why Human Beings Need the Virtues* (1999).

J. L. Mackie (1917–81) was an Australian philosopher specializing in truth and meta-ethics. His primary contribution is considered to be his work on ethical anti-realism in *Ethics: Inventing Right and Wrong* (1977).

John Stuart Mill (1806–73) was an English philosopher and legal reformer who studied under Jeremy Bentham and developed his theory of utilitarianism.

G. E. Moore (1873–1958) was an English philosopher famous in Cambridge for an argument called the "naturalistic fallacy," purporting to show that value terms like "good" are not reducible to natural terms like feelings of pleasure.

Iris Murdoch (1919–99) was an Irish-born British philosopher and novelist. Her philosophical work was based around a platonic realism about the good.

Kai Nielsen (b. 1926) is a moral philosopher and professor emeritus at the University of Calgary. His books include *Ethics without God* (1971).

Patrick Nowell-Smith (1914–2006) was an English moral philosopher and utilitarian. His most important work is *Ethics* (1956).

Martha Nussbaum (b. 1947) is the Ernst Freund Distinguished Service Professor of Law and Ethics at the University of Chicago. She is author of *The Fragility of Goodness* (1986) and *Upheavals of Thought: The Intelligence of Emotions* (2001), and she seeks to complement Kantian ethics with Aristotle.

Anthony O'Hear is a British philosopher, professor at Buckingham University, and director of the Royal Institute for Philosophy. His works include *After Progress* (1999).

Plato (c. 427–347 B.C.E.) was one of the most important philosophers in history. A disciple of Socrates, his dialogues cover most of the basic issues across the entire range of philosophical discourse—covering ethics, politics, knowledge, and God.

Philip L. Quinn (1940–2004) was a philosopher and theologian, noted as a scholar of the philosophy of physics and of ethics.

John Rawls (1921–2002) was a Harvard University professor and one of the most influential political philosophers of the twentieth century. His masterpiece, *A Theory of Justice*, published in 1971, forms the foundation of much contemporary liberal political theory.

D. J. Richter is a moral philosopher at Virginia Military Institute and author of *Ethics after Anscombe* (2000) and *Anscombe's Moral Philosophy* (2011).

Amartya Sen (b. 1933) is an Indian economist and Nobel laureate. He introduced the concept of welfare economics based on the capabilities approach that is influenced by virtue ethics.

Henry Sidgwick (1838–1900) was an English utilitarian philosopher and economist who promoted higher education for women. He is no longer widely known.

Peter Singer (b. 1946) is an Australian moral philosopher. He is perhaps the world's foremost utilitarian, and his books include *Practical Ethics* (1979) and *Animal Liberation: A New Ethics for Our Treatment of Animals* (1975).

Harry S. Truman (1884–1972) was the 33rd president of the United States, 1945–53. He forced the surrender of the Japanese in World War II by authorizing the nuclear devastation of Hiroshima and Nagasaki, which resulted in the deaths of hundreds of thousands of people.

Bernard Williams (1929–2003) was an English philosopher most noted for the concept of moral luck, whereby the moral value of an action can depend on things outside the agent's control.

Ludwig Wittgenstein (1889–1951) was an Austrian-born philosopher who worked mainly in England. His posthumously published master work *Philosophical Investigations* (1953) was collated and translated from German to English by his star student Elizabeth Anscombe and was enormously influential in British twentieth-century philosophy.

WORKS CITED

WORKS CITED

Adams, Robert. *Finite and Infinite Goods: A Framework for Ethics*. Oxford: Oxford University Press, 2002.

Anscombe, G. E. M. "Action, Intention and 'Double-Effect'." *Proceedings of the American Catholic Philosophical Association* 56 (1982): 12–25.

———. *Causality and Determination: An Inaugural Lecture*. Cambridge: Cambridge University Press, 1971.

———. *Contraception and Chastity*. London: Catholic Truth Society, 1975.

———. *Ethics, Religion and Politics*. Oxford: Basil Blackwell, 1981.

———. *Human Life, Action and Ethics*. St. Andrews Studies in Philosophy and Public Policy. Edited by Mary Geach and Luke Gormally. Exeter: Imprint Academic, 2005. Kindle edition.

———. *Intention*. Oxford: Basil Blackwell, 1957.

———. "Modern Moral Philosophy." *Philosophy* 33, no. 124 (1958): 1–19.

———. "A Note on Mr. Bennett." *Analysis* 26, no. 6 (1966): 208.

Aristotle. *Nicomachean Ethics.* Edited and translated by Roger Crisp. Cambridge: Cambridge University Press, 2014.

Austin, Michael W., ed. *Virtues in Action: New Essays in Applied Virtue Ethics*. Basingstoke: Palgrave Macmillan, 2013.

Ayer, A.J. *Language, Truth and Logic*. London: Victor Gollancz, 1936.

Bennett, Jonathan. *The Act Itself* . New York: Oxford University Press, 1995.

———. "Morality and Consequences." In *The Tanner Lectures on Human Values*, vol. 2, edited by Sterling McMurrin, 110-11. Salt Lake City: University of Utah Press, 1981.

———. "Whatever the Consequences." *Analysis* 26, no. 2 (1966): 83–102.

Bentham, Jeremy. *An Introduction to the Principles of Morals and Legislation*. Oxford: Clarendon Press, 1907.

Blackburn, Simon. "Against Anscombe: Review of *Human Life, Action and Ethics*." *Times Literary Supplement*, September 30, 2005: 11–12.

Conradi, Peter J. *Iris Murdoch: A Life*. London: HarperCollins, 2002.

Crisp, Roger. "Does Moral Philosophy Rest on a Mistake?", *Royal Institute of Philosophy Supplement* 54 (March 2004): 75–93. Accessed October 7, 2015. doi: 10.1017/S1358246100008456.

Driver, Julia. "Gertrude Elizabeth Margaret Anscombe." In *Stanford Encyclopedia of Philosophy* (Winter 2014 edition), edited by Edward N. Zalta. Accessed October 6, 2015. http://plato.stanford.edu/entries/anscombe/.

— — —. "The History of Utilitarianism." In *Stanford Encyclopedia of Philosophy* (Winter 2014 edition), edited by Edward N. Zalta. Accessed October 6, 2015. http://plato.stanford.edu/entries/utilitarianism-history/.

Foot, Philippa. *Natural Goodness*. Oxford: Oxford University Press, 2001.

— — —. *Virtue and Vices and Other Essays in Moral Philosophy*. Berkeley and Los Angeles: University of California Press, 1978.

Frankena, William K. "The Ethics of Love Conceived as an Ethics of Virtue." *Journal of Religious Ethics* 1 (Fall 1973): 21–36.

Fricker, Miranda. *Epistemic Injustice: Power and the Ethics of Knowing*. Oxford: Oxford University Press, 2007.

Geach, Peter T. *The Virtues*. Cambridge: Cambridge University Press, 1977.

Hauerwas, Stanley. *Character and the Christian Life*. San Antonio, TX: Trinity University Press, 1975.

— — —. "Obligation and Virtue Once More." *Journal of Religious Ethics* 3, no. 1 (Spring 1975): 27–44.

Hume, David. *Treatise of Human Nature*. Edited by L. A. Selby-Bigge and P. H. Nidditch. 2nd edition. Oxford: Oxford University Press, 1978.

Hursthouse, Rosalind. *Beginning Lives*. Oxford: Basil Blackwell in association with the Open University, 1987.

— — —. *On Virtue Ethics*. Oxford: Oxford University Press: 2001.

— — —. "Virtue Theory and Abortion." *Philosophy and Public Affairs* 20, no. 3 (1991): 223–46.

Korsgaard, Christine. *The Sources of Normativity*. Cambridge: Cambridge University Press, 1996.

Lazari-Radek, Katarzyna de and Peter Singer. *The Point of View of the Universe: Sidgwick and Contemporary Ethics*. Oxford: Oxford University Press, 2014.

MacIntyre, Alasdair. *After Virtue.* 3rd revised edition. London: Duckworth, 2007.

— — —. *Dependent Rational Animals*. London: Duckworth, 1999.

Murdoch, Iris. *The Sovereignty of Good*. London: Routledge & Kegan Paul, 1970.

Nielsen, Kai. "Some Remarks on the Independence of Morality from Religion." *Mind* 70, no. 278 (1961): 175–86.

Nietzsche, Friedrich Wilhelm. *Beyond Good and Evil: Prelude to a Philosophy of the Future.* Translated by R. J. Hollingdale. Harmondsworth: Penguin, 1990.

———. *On the Genealogy of Morals: A Polemic: By Way of Clarification and Supplement to My Last Book Beyond Good and Evil*. Translated by Douglas Smith. Oxford: Oxford University Press, 1996.

Nussbaum, Martha. *Upheavals of Thought: The Intelligence of Emotions*. Cambridge: Cambridge University Press, 2001.

O'Hear, Anthony, ed. *Modern Moral Philosophy: Royal Institute of Philosophy Supplement 54*. Cambridge: Cambridge University Press, 2004.

Pink, Thomas. "Moral Obligation." in *Modern Moral Philosophy: Royal Institute of Philosophy Supplement 54*, ed. Anthony O'Hear. Cambridge: Cambridge University Press, 2004, 159–69.

Plato, *Euthyphro*. In *Readings in Ancient Greek Philosophy*, 2nd edition, edited by S. Marc Cohen and Patricia Curd, translated by C. D. C. Reeve, 97–114. Indianapolis: Hackett Publishing, 2005.

Quinn, Philip. *Divine Commands and Moral Requirements*. Oxford: Clarendon Library of Logic and Philosophy, 1978.

Rawls, John. *A Theory of Justice*. Cambridge, MA: Harvard University Press, 1971.

Richter, D. J. *Ethics after Anscombe: Post "Modern Moral Philosophy"*. Dordrecht: Springer Publishers, 2000.

Russell, Daniel C., ed. *The Cambridge Companion to Virtue Ethics*. Cambridge: Cambridge University Press, 2013.

Schultz, Barton. "Henry Sidgwick." In *The Stanford Encyclopedia of Philosophy* (Summer 2015 edition), edited by Edward N. Zalta. Accessed October 7, 2015. http://stanford.library.usyd.edu.au/archives/sum2010/entries/sidgwick/.

Sidgwick, Henry. *Methods of Ethics*, 7th edition. Indianapolis: Hackett, 1981.

Singer, Peter. *Practical Ethics*. Cambridge: Cambridge University Press, 1979.

Sinnott-Armstrong, Walter, ed. *Moral Psychology. Vol. 1. The Evolution of Morality: Adaptations and Innateness*. Cambridge, MA: MIT, 2007.

Teichmann, Roger. *The Philosophy of Elizabeth Anscombe*. Oxford: Oxford University Press, 2008.

Williams, Bernard and J. J. C. Smart. *Utilitarianism: For and Against*. Cambridge: Cambridge University Press, 1973.

Wittgenstein, Ludwig. *Philosophical Investigations (Philosophische Untersuchungen) English & German*, trans. G. E. M. Anscombe. Oxford: Basil Blackwell, 1953).

— — —. *Philosophical Investigations*, 4th edition, 2009. Edited and translated by P. M. S. Hacker and Joachim Schulte. Oxford: Wiley-Blackwell, 2009.

— — —. *Tractatus Logico-Philosophicus*. Translated by D. F. Pears and B. F. McGuinness. London: Routledge & Kegan Paul, 1974.

THE MACAT LIBRARY
BY DISCIPLINE

AFRICANA STUDIES

Chinua Achebe's *An Image of Africa: Racism in Conrad's Heart of Darkness*
W. E. B. Du Bois's *The Souls of Black Folk*
Zora Neale Huston's *Characteristics of Negro Expression*
Martin Luther King Jr's *Why We Can't Wait*
Toni Morrison's *Playing in the Dark: Whiteness in the American Literary Imagination*

ANTHROPOLOGY

Arjun Appadurai's *Modernity at Large: Cultural Dimensions of Globalisation*
Philippe Ariès's *Centuries of Childhood*
Franz Boas's *Race, Language and Culture*
Kim Chan & Renée Mauborgne's *Blue Ocean Strategy*
Jared Diamond's *Guns, Germs & Steel: the Fate of Human Societies*
Jared Diamond's *Collapse: How Societies Choose to Fail or Survive*
E. E. Evans-Pritchard's *Witchcraft, Oracles and Magic Among the Azande*
James Ferguson's *The Anti-Politics Machine*
Clifford Geertz's *The Interpretation of Cultures*
David Graeber's *Debt: the First 5000 Years*
Karen Ho's *Liquidated: An Ethnography of Wall Street*
Geert Hofstede's *Culture's Consequences: Comparing Values, Behaviors, Institutes and Organizations across Nations*
Claude Lévi-Strauss's *Structural Anthropology*
Jay Macleod's *Ain't No Makin' It: Aspirations and Attainment in a Low-Income Neighborhood*
Saba Mahmood's *The Politics of Piety: The Islamic Revival and the Feminist Subjec*t
Marcel Mauss's *The Gift*

BUSINESS

Jean Lave & Etienne Wenger's *Situated Learning*
Theodore Levitt's *Marketing Myopia*
Burton G. Malkiel's *A Random Walk Down Wall Street*
Douglas McGregor's *The Human Side of Enterprise*
Michael Porter's *Competitive Strategy: Creating and Sustaining Superior Performance*
John Kotter's *Leading Change*
C. K. Prahalad & Gary Hamel's *The Core Competence of the Corporation*

CRIMINOLOGY

Michelle Alexander's *The New Jim Crow: Mass Incarceration in the Age of Colorblindness*
Michael R. Gottfredson & Travis Hirschi's *A General Theory of Crime*
Richard Herrnstein & Charles A. Murray's *The Bell Curve: Intelligence and Class Structure in American Life*
Elizabeth Loftus's *Eyewitness Testimony*
Jay Macleod's *Ain't No Makin' It: Aspirations and Attainment in a Low-Income Neighborhood*
Philip Zimbardo's *The Lucifer Effect*

ECONOMICS

Janet Abu-Lughod's *Before European Hegemony*
Ha-Joon Chang's *Kicking Away the Ladder*
David Brion Davis's *The Problem of Slavery in the Age of Revolution*
Milton Friedman's *The Role of Monetary Policy*
Milton Friedman's *Capitalism and Freedom*
David Graeber's *Debt: the First 5000 Years*
Friedrich Hayek's *The Road to Serfdom*
Karen Ho's *Liquidated: An Ethnography of Wall Street*

The Macat Library By Discipline

John Maynard Keynes's *The General Theory of Employment, Interest and Money*
Charles P. Kindleberger's *Manias, Panics and Crashes*
Robert Lucas's *Why Doesn't Capital Flow from Rich to Poor Countries?*
Burton G. Malkiel's *A Random Walk Down Wall Street*
Thomas Robert Malthus's *An Essay on the Principle of Population*
Karl Marx's *Capital*
Thomas Piketty's *Capital in the Twenty-First Century*
Amartya Sen's *Development as Freedom*
Adam Smith's *The Wealth of Nations*
Nassim Nicholas Taleb's *The Black Swan: The Impact of the Highly Improbable*
Amos Tversky's & Daniel Kahneman's *Judgment under Uncertainty: Heuristics and Biases*
Mahbub Ul Haq's *Reflections on Human Development*
Max Weber's *The Protestant Ethic and the Spirit of Capitalism*

FEMINISM AND GENDER STUDIES

Judith Butler's *Gender Trouble*
Simone De Beauvoir's *The Second Sex*
Michel Foucault's *History of Sexuality*
Betty Friedan's *The Feminine Mystique*
Saba Mahmood's *The Politics of Piety: The Islamic Revival and the Feminist Subject*
Joan Wallach Scott's *Gender and the Politics of History*
Mary Wollstonecraft's *A Vindication of the Rights of Woman*
Virginia Woolf's *A Room of One's Own*

GEOGRAPHY

The Brundtland Report's *Our Common Future*
Rachel Carson's *Silent Spring*
Charles Darwin's *On the Origin of Species*
James Ferguson's *The Anti-Politics Machine*
Jane Jacobs's *The Death and Life of Great American Cities*
James Lovelock's *Gaia: A New Look at Life on Earth*
Amartya Sen's *Development as Freedom*
Mathis Wackernagel & William Rees's *Our Ecological Footprint*

HISTORY

Janet Abu-Lughod's *Before European Hegemony*
Benedict Anderson's *Imagined Communities*
Bernard Bailyn's *The Ideological Origins of the American Revolution*
Hanna Batatu's *The Old Social Classes And The Revolutionary Movements Of Iraq*
Christopher Browning's *Ordinary Men: Reserve Police Batallion 101 and the Final Solution in Poland*
Edmund Burke's *Reflections on the Revolution in France*
William Cronon's *Nature's Metropolis: Chicago And The Great West*
Alfred W. Crosby's *The Columbian Exchange*
Hamid Dabashi's *Iran: A People Interrupted*
David Brion Davis's *The Problem of Slavery in the Age of Revolution*
Nathalie Zemon Davis's *The Return of Martin Guerre*
Jared Diamond's *Guns, Germs & Steel: the Fate of Human Societies*
Frank Dikotter's *Mao's Great Famine*
John W Dower's *War Without Mercy: Race And Power In The Pacific War*
W. E. B. Du Bois's *The Souls of Black Folk*
Richard J. Evans's *In Defence of History*
Lucien Febvre's *The Problem of Unbelief in the 16th Century*
Sheila Fitzpatrick's *Everyday Stalinism*

Eric Foner's *Reconstruction: America's Unfinished Revolution, 1863-1877*
Michel Foucault's *Discipline and Punish*
Michel Foucault's *History of Sexuality*
Francis Fukuyama's *The End of History and the Last Man*
John Lewis Gaddis's *We Now Know: Rethinking Cold War History*
Ernest Gellner's *Nations and Nationalism*
Eugene Genovese's *Roll, Jordan, Roll: The World the Slaves Made*
Carlo Ginzburg's *The Night Battles*
Daniel Goldhagen's *Hitler's Willing Executioners*
Jack Goldstone's *Revolution and Rebellion in the Early Modern World*
Antonio Gramsci's *The Prison Notebooks*
Alexander Hamilton, John Jay & James Madison's *The Federalist Papers*
Christopher Hill's *The World Turned Upside Down*
Carole Hillenbrand's *The Crusades: Islamic Perspectives*
Thomas Hobbes's *Leviathan*
Eric Hobsbawm's *The Age Of Revolution*
John A. Hobson's *Imperialism: A Study*
Albert Hourani's *History of the Arab Peoples*
Samuel P. Huntington's *The Clash of Civilizations and the Remaking of World Order*
C. L. R. James's *The Black Jacobins*
Tony Judt's *Postwar: A History of Europe Since 1945*
Ernst Kantorowicz's *The King's Two Bodies: A Study in Medieval Political Theology*
Paul Kennedy's *The Rise and Fall of the Great Powers*
Ian Kershaw's *The "Hitler Myth": Image and Reality in the Third Reich*
John Maynard Keynes's *The General Theory of Employment, Interest and Money*
Charles P. Kindleberger's *Manias, Panics and Crashes*
Martin Luther King Jr's *Why We Can't Wait*
Henry Kissinger's *World Order: Reflections on the Character of Nations and the Course of History*
Thomas Kuhn's *The Structure of Scientific Revolutions*
Georges Lefebvre's *The Coming of the French Revolution*
John Locke's *Two Treatises of Government*
Niccolò Machiavelli's *The Prince*
Thomas Robert Malthus's *An Essay on the Principle of Population*
Mahmood Mamdani's *Citizen and Subject: Contemporary Africa And The Legacy Of Late Colonialism*
Karl Marx's *Capital*
Stanley Milgram's *Obedience to Authority*
John Stuart Mill's *On Liberty*
Thomas Paine's *Common Sense*
Thomas Paine's *Rights of Man*
Geoffrey Parker's *Global Crisis: War, Climate Change and Catastrophe in the Seventeenth Century*
Jonathan Riley-Smith's *The First Crusade and the Idea of Crusading*
Jean-Jacques Rousseau's *The Social Contract*
Joan Wallach Scott's *Gender and the Politics of History*
Theda Skocpol's *States and Social Revolutions*
Adam Smith's *The Wealth of Nations*
Timothy Snyder's *Bloodlands: Europe Between Hitler and Stalin*
Sun Tzu's *The Art of War*
Keith Thomas's *Religion and the Decline of Magic*
Thucydides's *The History of the Peloponnesian War*
Frederick Jackson Turner's *The Significance of the Frontier in American History*
Odd Arne Westad's *The Global Cold War: Third World Interventions And The Making Of Our Times*

LITERATURE

Chinua Achebe's *An Image of Africa: Racism in Conrad's Heart of Darkness*
Roland Barthes's *Mythologies*
Homi K. Bhabha's *The Location of Culture*
Judith Butler's *Gender Trouble*
Simone De Beauvoir's *The Second Sex*
Ferdinand De Saussure's *Course in General Linguistics*
T. S. Eliot's *The Sacred Wood: Essays on Poetry and Criticism*
Zora Neale Huston's *Characteristics of Negro Expression*
Toni Morrison's *Playing in the Dark: Whiteness in the American Literary Imagination*
Edward Said's *Orientalism*
Gayatri Chakravorty Spivak's *Can the Subaltern Speak?*
Mary Wollstonecraft's *A Vindication of the Rights of Women*
Virginia Woolf's *A Room of One's Own*

PHILOSOPHY

Elizabeth Anscombe's *Modern Moral Philosophy*
Hannah Arendt's *The Human Condition*
Aristotle's *Metaphysics*
Aristotle's *Nicomachean Ethics*
Edmund Gettier's *Is Justified True Belief Knowledge?*
Georg Wilhelm Friedrich Hegel's *Phenomenology of Spirit*
David Hume's *Dialogues Concerning Natural Religion*
David Hume's *The Enquiry for Human Understanding*
Immanuel Kant's *Religion within the Boundaries of Mere Reason*
Immanuel Kant's *Critique of Pure Reason*
Søren Kierkegaard's *The Sickness Unto Death*
Søren Kierkegaard's *Fear and Trembling*
C. S. Lewis's *The Abolition of Man*
Alasdair MacIntyre's *After Virtue*
Marcus Aurelius's *Meditations*
Friedrich Nietzsche's *On the Genealogy of Morality*
Friedrich Nietzsche's *Beyond Good and Evil*
Plato's *Republic*
Plato's *Symposium*
Jean-Jacques Rousseau's *The Social Contract*
Gilbert Ryle's *The Concept of Mind*
Baruch Spinoza's *Ethics*
Sun Tzu's *The Art of War*
Ludwig Wittgenstein's *Philosophical Investigations*

POLITICS

Benedict Anderson's *Imagined Communities*
Aristotle's *Politics*
Bernard Bailyn's *The Ideological Origins of the American Revolution*
Edmund Burke's *Reflections on the Revolution in France*
John C. Calhoun's *A Disquisition on Government*
Ha-Joon Chang's *Kicking Away the Ladder*
Hamid Dabashi's *Iran: A People Interrupted*
Hamid Dabashi's *Theology of Discontent: The Ideological Foundation of the Islamic Revolution in Iran*
Robert Dahl's *Democracy and its Critics*
Robert Dahl's *Who Governs?*
David Brion Davis's *The Problem of Slavery in the Age of Revolution*

Alexis De Tocqueville's *Democracy in America*
James Ferguson's *The Anti-Politics Machine*
Frank Dikotter's *Mao's Great Famine*
Sheila Fitzpatrick's *Everyday Stalinism*
Eric Foner's *Reconstruction: America's Unfinished Revolution, 1863-1877*
Milton Friedman's *Capitalism and Freedom*
Francis Fukuyama's *The End of History and the Last Man*
John Lewis Gaddis's *We Now Know: Rethinking Cold War History*
Ernest Gellner's *Nations and Nationalism*
David Graeber's *Debt: the First 5000 Years*
Antonio Gramsci's *The Prison Notebooks*
Alexander Hamilton, John Jay & James Madison's *The Federalist Papers*
Friedrich Hayek's *The Road to Serfdom*
Christopher Hill's *The World Turned Upside Down*
Thomas Hobbes's *Leviathan*
John A. Hobson's *Imperialism: A Study*
Samuel P. Huntington's *The Clash of Civilizations and the Remaking of World Order*
Tony Judt's *Postwar: A History of Europe Since 1945*
David C. Kang's *China Rising: Peace, Power and Order in East Asia*
Paul Kennedy's *The Rise and Fall of Great Powers*
Robert Keohane's *After Hegemony*
Martin Luther King Jr.'s *Why We Can't Wait*
Henry Kissinger's *World Order: Reflections on the Character of Nations and the Course of History*
John Locke's *Two Treatises of Government*
Niccolò Machiavelli's *The Prince*
Thomas Robert Malthus's *An Essay on the Principle of Population*
Mahmood Mamdani's *Citizen and Subject: Contemporary Africa And The Legacy Of Late Colonialism*
Karl Marx's *Capital*
John Stuart Mill's *On Liberty*
John Stuart Mill's *Utilitarianism*
Hans Morgenthau's *Politics Among Nations*
Thomas Paine's *Common Sense*
Thomas Paine's *Rights of Man*
Thomas Piketty's *Capital in the Twenty-First Century*
Robert D. Putnam's *Bowling Alone*
John Rawls's *Theory of Justice*
Jean-Jacques Rousseau's *The Social Contract*
Theda Skocpol's *States and Social Revolutions*
Adam Smith's *The Wealth of Nations*
Sun Tzu's *The Art of War*
Henry David Thoreau's *Civil Disobedience*
Thucydides's *The History of the Peloponnesian War*
Kenneth Waltz's *Theory of International Politics*
Max Weber's *Politics as a Vocation*
Odd Arne Westad's *The Global Cold War: Third World Interventions And The Making Of Our Times*

POSTCOLONIAL STUDIES

Roland Barthes's *Mythologies*
Frantz Fanon's *Black Skin, White Masks*
Homi K. Bhabha's *The Location of Culture*
Gustavo Gutiérrez's *A Theology of Liberation*
Edward Said's *Orientalism*
Gayatri Chakravorty Spivak's *Can the Subaltern Speak?*

PSYCHOLOGY

Gordon Allport's *The Nature of Prejudice*
Alan Baddeley & Graham Hitch's *Aggression: A Social Learning Analysis*
Albert Bandura's *Aggression: A Social Learning Analysis*
Leon Festinger's *A Theory of Cognitive Dissonance*
Sigmund Freud's *The Interpretation of Dreams*
Betty Friedan's *The Feminine Mystique*
Michael R. Gottfredson & Travis Hirschi's *A General Theory of Crime*
Eric Hoffer's *The True Believer: Thoughts on the Nature of Mass Movements*
William James's *Principles of Psychology*
Elizabeth Loftus's *Eyewitness Testimony*
A. H. Maslow's *A Theory of Human Motivation*
Stanley Milgram's *Obedience to Authority*
Steven Pinker's *The Better Angels of Our Nature*
Oliver Sacks's *The Man Who Mistook His Wife For a Hat*
Richard Thaler & Cass Sunstein's *Nudge: Improving Decisions About Health, Wealth and Happiness*
Amos Tversky's *Judgment under Uncertainty: Heuristics and Biases*
Philip Zimbardo's *The Lucifer Effect*

SCIENCE

Rachel Carson's *Silent Spring*
William Cronon's *Nature's Metropolis: Chicago And The Great West*
Alfred W. Crosby's *The Columbian Exchange*
Charles Darwin's *On the Origin of Species*
Richard Dawkin's *The Selfish Gene*
Thomas Kuhn's *The Structure of Scientific Revolutions*
Geoffrey Parker's *Global Crisis: War, Climate Change and Catastrophe in the Seventeenth Century*
Mathis Wackernagel & William Rees's *Our Ecological Footprint*

SOCIOLOGY

Michelle Alexander's *The New Jim Crow: Mass Incarceration in the Age of Colorblindness*
Gordon Allport's *The Nature of Prejudice*
Albert Bandura's *Aggression: A Social Learning Analysis*
Hanna Batatu's *The Old Social Classes And The Revolutionary Movements Of Iraq*
Ha-Joon Chang's *Kicking Away the Ladder*
W. E. B. Du Bois's *The Souls of Black Folk*
Émile Durkheim's *On Suicide*
Frantz Fanon's *Black Skin, White Masks*
Frantz Fanon's *The Wretched of the Earth*
Eric Foner's *Reconstruction: America's Unfinished Revolution, 1863-1877*
Eugene Genovese's *Roll, Jordan, Roll: The World the Slaves Made*
Jack Goldstone's *Revolution and Rebellion in the Early Modern World*
Antonio Gramsci's *The Prison Notebooks*
Richard Herrnstein & Charles A Murray's *The Bell Curve: Intelligence and Class Structure in American Life*
Eric Hoffer's *The True Believer: Thoughts on the Nature of Mass Movements*
Jane Jacobs's *The Death and Life of Great American Cities*
Robert Lucas's *Why Doesn't Capital Flow from Rich to Poor Countries?*
Jay Macleod's *Ain't No Makin' It: Aspirations and Attainment in a Low Income Neighborhood*
Elaine May's *Homeward Bound: American Families in the Cold War Era*
Douglas McGregor's *The Human Side of Enterprise*
C. Wright Mills's *The Sociological Imagination*

Thomas Piketty's *Capital in the Twenty-First Century*
Robert D. Putman's *Bowling Alone*
David Riesman's *The Lonely Crowd: A Study of the Changing American Character*
Edward Said's *Orientalism*
Joan Wallach Scott's *Gender and the Politics of History*
Theda Skocpol's *States and Social Revolutions*
Max Weber's *The Protestant Ethic and the Spirit of Capitalism*

THEOLOGY

Augustine's *Confessions*
Benedict's *Rule of St Benedict*
Gustavo Gutiérrez's *A Theology of Liberation*
Carole Hillenbrand's *The Crusades: Islamic Perspectives*
David Hume's *Dialogues Concerning Natural Religion*
Immanuel Kant's *Religion within the Boundaries of Mere Reason*
Ernst Kantorowicz's *The King's Two Bodies: A Study in Medieval Political Theology*
Søren Kierkegaard's *The Sickness Unto Death*
C. S. Lewis's *The Abolition of Man*
Saba Mahmood's *The Politics of Piety: The Islamic Revival and the Feminist Subject*
Baruch Spinoza's *Ethics*
Keith Thomas's *Religion and the Decline of Magic*

COMING SOON

Chris Argyris's *The Individual and the Organisation*
Seyla Benhabib's *The Rights of Others*
Walter Benjamin's *The Work Of Art in the Age of Mechanical Reproduction*
John Berger's *Ways of Seeing*
Pierre Bourdieu's *Outline of a Theory of Practice*
Mary Douglas's *Purity and Danger*
Roland Dworkin's *Taking Rights Seriously*
James G. March's *Exploration and Exploitation in Organisational Learning*
Ikujiro Nonaka's *A Dynamic Theory of Organizational Knowledge Creation*
Griselda Pollock's *Vision and Difference*
Amartya Sen's *Inequality Re-Examined*
Susan Sontag's *On Photography*
Yasser Tabbaa's *The Transformation of Islamic Art*
Ludwig von Mises's *Theory of Money and Credit*

Macat Disciplines

Access the greatest ideas and thinkers across entire disciplines, including

Postcolonial Studies

Roland Barthes's *Mythologies*
Frantz Fanon's *Black Skin, White Masks*
Homi K. Bhabha's *The Location of Culture*
Gustavo Gutiérrez's *A Theology of Liberation*
Edward Said's *Orientalism*
Gayatri Chakravorty Spivak's *Can the Subaltern Speak?*

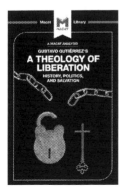

Macat analyses are available from all good bookshops and libraries.

Access hundreds of analyses through one, multimedia tool.
Join free for one month **library.macat.com**

Macat Disciplines

Access the greatest ideas and thinkers across entire disciplines, including

AFRICANA STUDIES

Chinua Achebe's *An Image of Africa: Racism in Conrad's Heart of Darkness*

W. E. B. Du Bois's *The Souls of Black Folk*

Zora Neale Hurston's *Characteristics of Negro Expression*

Martin Luther King Jr.'s *Why We Can't Wait*

Toni Morrison's *Playing in the Dark: Whiteness in the American Literary Imagination*

Macat analyses are available from all good bookshops and libraries.

Access hundreds of analyses through one, multimedia tool.
Join free for one month **library.macat.com**

Macat Disciplines

Access the greatest ideas and thinkers across entire disciplines, including

FEMINISM, GENDER AND QUEER STUDIES

Simone De Beauvoir's
The Second Sex

Michel Foucault's
History of Sexuality

Betty Friedan's
The Feminine Mystique

Saba Mahmood's
*The Politics of Piety:
The Islamic Revival and
the Feminist Subject*

Joan Wallach Scott's
*Gender and the
Politics of History*

Mary Wollstonecraft's
*A Vindication of the
Rights of Woman*

Virginia Woolf's
A Room of One's Own

Judith Butler's
Gender Trouble

Macat analyses are available from all good bookshops and libraries.

Access hundreds of analyses through one, multimedia tool.
Join free for one month **library.macat.com**

Macat Disciplines

Access the greatest ideas and thinkers across entire disciplines, including

CRIMINOLOGY

Michelle Alexander's
The New Jim Crow: Mass Incarceration in the Age of Colorblindness

Michael R. Gottfredson & Travis Hirschi's
A General Theory of Crime

Elizabeth Loftus's
Eyewitness Testimony

Richard Herrnstein & Charles A. Murray's
The Bell Curve: Intelligence and Class Structure in American Life

Jay Macleod's
Ain't No Makin' It: Aspirations and Attainment in a Low-Income Neighborhood

Philip Zimbardo's
The Lucifer Effect

Macat Disciplines

Access the greatest ideas and thinkers across entire disciplines, including

INEQUALITY

Ha-Joon Chang's, *Kicking Away the Ladder*

David Graeber's, *Debt: The First 5000 Years*

Robert E. Lucas's, *Why Doesn't Capital Flow from Rich To Poor Countries?*

Thomas Piketty's, *Capital in the Twenty-First Century*

Amartya Sen's, *Inequality Re-Examined*

Mahbub Ul Haq's, *Reflections on Human Development*

Macat analyses are available from all good bookshops and libraries.

Access hundreds of analyses through one, multimedia tool.
Join free for one month **library.macat.com**

Macat Disciplines

*Access the greatest ideas and thinkers
across entire disciplines, including*

GLOBALIZATION

Arjun Appadurai's, *Modernity at Large:
Cultural Dimensions of Globalisation*

James Ferguson's, *The Anti-Politics Machine*

Geert Hofstede's, *Culture's Consequences*

Amartya Sen's, *Development as Freedom*

Macat analyses are available from all good bookshops and libraries.

Access hundreds of analyses through one, multimedia tool.
Join free for one month **library.macat.com**

Macat Disciplines

Access the greatest ideas and thinkers across entire disciplines, including

MAN AND THE ENVIRONMENT

The Brundtland Report's, *Our Common Future*
Rachel Carson's, *Silent Spring*
James Lovelock's, *Gaia: A New Look at Life on Earth*
Mathis Wackernagel & William Rees's, *Our Ecological Footprint*

Macat Disciplines

Access the greatest ideas and thinkers across entire disciplines, including

THE FUTURE OF DEMOCRACY

Robert A. Dahl's, *Democracy and Its Critics*
Robert A. Dahl's, *Who Governs?*
Alexis De Toqueville's, *Democracy in America*
Niccolò Machiavelli's, *The Prince*
John Stuart Mill's, *On Liberty*
Robert D. Putnam's, *Bowling Alone*
Jean-Jacques Rousseau's, *The Social Contract*
Henry David Thoreau's, *Civil Disobedience*

Macat Disciplines

Access the greatest ideas and thinkers
across entire disciplines, including

TOTALITARIANISM

Sheila Fitzpatrick's, *Everyday Stalinism*
Ian Kershaw's, *The "Hitler Myth"*
Timothy Snyder's, *Bloodlands*

Macat Pairs

Analyse historical and modern issues from opposite sides of an argument. Pairs include:

RACE AND IDENTITY

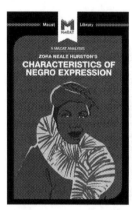

Zora Neale Hurston's
Characteristics of Negro Expression

Using material collected on anthropological expeditions to the South, Zora Neale Hurston explains how expression in African American culture in the early twentieth century departs from the art of white America. At the time, African American art was often criticized for copying white culture. For Hurston, this criticism misunderstood how art works. European tradition views art as something fixed. But Hurston describes a creative process that is alive, ever-changing, and largely improvisational. She maintains that African American art works through a process called 'mimicry'—where an imitated object or verbal pattern, for example, is reshaped and altered until it becomes something new, novel—and worthy of attention.

Frantz Fanon's
Black Skin, White Masks

Black Skin, White Masks offers a radical analysis of the psychological effects of colonization on the colonized.

Fanon witnessed the effects of colonization first hand both in his birthplace, Martinique, and again later in life when he worked as a psychiatrist in another French colony, Algeria. His text is uncompromising in form and argument. He dissects the dehumanizing effects of colonialism, arguing that it destroys the native sense of identity, forcing people to adapt to an alien set of values—including a core belief that they are inferior. This results in deep psychological trauma.

Fanon's work played a pivotal role in the civil rights movements of the 1960s.

Macat analyses are available from all good bookshops and libraries.

Access hundreds of analyses through one, multimedia tool.
Join free for one month **library.macat.com**

Macat Pairs

*Analyse historical and modern issues
from opposite sides of an argument.
Pairs include:*

INTERNATIONAL RELATIONS IN THE 21ST CENTURY

Samuel P. Huntington's
The Clash of Civilisations

In his highly influential 1996 book, Huntington offers a vision of a post-Cold War world in which conflict takes place not between competing ideologies but between cultures. The worst clash, he argues, will be between the Islamic world and the West: the West's arrogance and belief that its culture is a "gift" to the world will come into conflict with Islam's obstinacy and concern that its culture is under attack from a morally decadent "other."

Clash inspired much debate between different political schools of thought. But its greatest impact came in helping define American foreign policy in the wake of the 2001 terrorist attacks in New York and Washington.

Francis Fukuyama's
The End of History and the Last Man

Published in 1992, *The End of History and the Last Man* argues that capitalist democracy is the final destination for all societies. Fukuyama believed democracy triumphed during the Cold War because it lacks the "fundamental contradictions" inherent in communism and satisfies our yearning for freedom and equality. Democracy therefore marks the endpoint in the evolution of ideology, and so the "end of history." There will still be "events," but no fundamental change in ideology.

Macat Pairs

Analyse historical and modern issues from opposite sides of an argument. Pairs include:

HOW TO RUN AN ECONOMY

John Maynard Keynes's
The General Theory OF Employment, Interest and Money

Classical economics suggests that market economies are self-correcting in times of recession or depression, and tend toward full employment and output. But English economist John Maynard Keynes disagrees.

In his ground-breaking 1936 study *The General Theory*, Keynes argues that traditional economics has misunderstood the causes of unemployment. Employment is not determined by the price of labor; it is directly linked to demand. Keynes believes market economies are by nature unstable, and so require government intervention. Spurred on by the social catastrophe of the Great Depression of the 1930s, he sets out to revolutionize the way the world thinks

Milton Friedman's
The Role of Monetary Policy

Friedman's 1968 paper changed the course of economic theory. In just 17 pages, he demolished existing theory and outlined an effective alternate monetary policy designed to secure 'high employment, stable prices and rapid growth.'

Friedman demonstrated that monetary policy plays a vital role in broader economic stability and argued that economists got their monetary policy wrong in the 1950s and 1960s by misunderstanding the relationship between inflation and unemployment. Previous generations of economists had believed that governments could permanently decrease unemployment by permitting inflation—and vice versa. Friedman's most original contribution was to show that this supposed trade-off is an illusion that only works in the short term.

Macat analyses are available from all good bookshops and libraries.

Access hundreds of analyses through one, multimedia tool.
Join free for one month **library.macat.com**

Macat Pairs

Analyse historical and modern issues
from opposite sides of an argument.
Pairs include:

ARE WE FUNDAMENTALLY GOOD - OR BAD?

Steven Pinker's
The Better Angels of Our Nature

Stephen Pinker's gloriously optimistic 2011 book argues that, despite humanity's biological tendency toward violence, we are, in fact, less violent today than ever before. To prove his case, Pinker lays out pages of detailed statistical evidence. For him, much of the credit for the decline goes to the eighteenth-century Enlightenment movement, whose ideas of liberty, tolerance, and respect for the value of human life filtered down through society and affected how people thought. That psychological change led to behavioral change—and overall we became more peaceful. Critics countered that humanity could never overcome the biological urge toward violence; others argued that Pinker's statistics were flawed.

Philip Zimbardo's
The Lucifer Effect

Some psychologists believe those who commit cruelty are innately evil. Zimbardo disagrees. In *The Lucifer Effect*, he argues that sometimes good people do evil things simply because of the situations they find themselves in, citing many historical examples to illustrate his point. Zimbardo details his 1971 Stanford prison experiment, where ordinary volunteers playing guards in a mock prison rapidly became abusive. But he also describes the tortures committed by US army personnel in Iraq's Abu Ghraib prison in 2003—and how he himself testified in defence of one of those guards. committed by US army personnel in Iraq's Abu Ghraib prison in 2003—and how he himself testified in defence of one of those guards.

Macat analyses are available from all good bookshops and libraries.

Access hundreds of analyses through one, multimedia tool.
Join free for one month **library.macat.com**

Macat Pairs

Analyse historical and modern issues from opposite sides of an argument. Pairs include:

HOW WE RELATE TO EACH OTHER AND SOCIETY

Jean-Jacques Rousseau's
The Social Contract

Rousseau's famous work sets out the radical concept of the 'social contract': a give-and-take relationship between individual freedom and social order.

If people are free to do as they like, governed only by their own sense of justice, they are also vulnerable to chaos and violence. To avoid this, Rousseau proposes, they should agree to give up some freedom to benefit from the protection of social and political organization. But this deal is only just if societies are led by the collective needs and desires of the people, and able to control the private interests of individuals. For Rousseau, the only legitimate form of government is rule by the people.

Robert D. Putnam's
Bowling Alone

In *Bowling Alone*, Robert Putnam argues that Americans have become disconnected from one another and from the institutions of their common life, and investigates the consequences of this change.

Looking at a range of indicators, from membership in formal organizations to the number of invitations being extended to informal dinner parties, Putnam demonstrates that Americans are interacting less and creating less "social capital" – with potentially disastrous implications for their society.

It would be difficult to overstate the impact of *Bowling Alone*, one of the most frequently cited social science publications of the last half-century.

Printed in the United States
by Baker & Taylor Publisher Services